T0128288

LIFE'S ROADWAYS *are* FULL *of* LEFT TURNS

DAWN GREGORY

WESTBOW
PRESS®
A DIVISION OF THOMAS NELSON
& ZONDERVAN

WestBow Press books may be ordered through booksellers or by contacting:

WestBow Press
A Division of Thomas Nelson & Zondervan
1663 Liberty Drive
Bloomington, IN 47403
www.westbowpress.com
844-714-3454

ISBN: 978-1-6642-9265-9 (sc)
ISBN: 978-1-6642-9266-6 (hc)
ISBN: 978-1-6642-9267-3 (e)

Library of Congress Control Number: 2023903094

Print information available on the last page.

WestBow Press rev. date: 02/14/2023

To the reader:

My dream has always been to write. I just never had a clear vision to do so. Encouragement and clarity from a dear friend gave me the push I needed. The journey started. And now, I just want to share it all with the world. The journey of finding my purpose. My walk to truly find my inner spirit, the light God has given me to shine. The profound testimony of the enlightenment I have been drawn to and share with others. We all have a past. We all have been in situations. We all have dealt with life events in different ways. Sometimes bringing all that to light gives us and others a good sense of who we are at this moment. Sharing moments of our lives can help others come to discover realizations about their own lives.

Which direction should I go? How do I know anything? Always wanting to live life to the fullest. Never knowing what is really behind each door. Open it. Close it. Lock it. Leave it wide open. Walk thru. It is never about knowing. Because I don't. It is always about learning. Mistakes will be made. Victories should be celebrated. Faith needs to be discovered. Heart and mind have to work together. Definitely not easy. Getting to the right place. Mentally. Emotionally. Spiritually. It all comes together. Patience is a requirement. Trust in God's plan a must. The pages ahead are all about my walk to find me, with (lots of) help, guidance, patience, and trust that I never thought I would find, especially the way I found it all.

I have always tried to be a good person. Wanting to do all the right things. Make others proud of me. Even with all those very real goals, I have always been insecure in all my abilities to come out on top. That was the wrong way to look at life. I am learning that now in so many different ways. My focus was about being accepted, liked, and never wanting to disappoint. It should have been about being true to myself, trusting God above man, and having faith God would always lead me. But as we all know, there are so many things in front of us which misleads the mind and heart. I, for some reason, put my trust in man because that is what has always been right in front of me. I felt having relationships with people was more important than having a strong relationship with God. I realize now how wrong that mindset was then. People have let me down so many times, but God has always been there. Maybe I was not as aware of the things God was doing in my life when He was working so hard to make me see. I guess I wanted what I wanted mistakenly thinking I knew what was best. I don't. But I am learning how to make sure I am on the path God wants me on now. And that is where I want to stay.

How did I finally get here? That is a question with many answers. I will try to make it all easy to understand.

I grew up going to church. My parents and family made it seem normal to get up on Sunday, put a dress on, go sit in church for an hour or so, and behave. There was also Sunday school if we got up early enough. I can't say I remember too much of my church experience before the age of 10. There were stories told and I listened, but pretty sure I did not process it. Knowing the difference between right and wrong was easy. The Ten Commandments shoved at you and being told to memorize them. Bible verses we had to repeat word for word and know the 'right' meaning according to the person in charge of the group discussing it. Told I had to know all the books of the Bible in order and how to spell them. Those are the things I remember about church or children's activities at church. It was a little disheartening to me. I did the best I could, but was not very good at memorizing anything I did not use everyday. (And I'm still not.) But at church or during church 'school' activities, I was told it was a must to know all these things or I could not move on to other classes or activities. So, I did what was expected of me cramming for every 'test' they threw at me. Not easy but I made it.

I have attended many types of churches over my lifetime. Each one had some kind of impact on me. I did what I was supposed to during all things church related. I enjoyed going to church for the most part. Loved the music and making friends. And there was a time I thought I might even want to become a minister/pastor. I always wanted to be able to make a difference in people's lives in some way. Church always gave me feelings that I could never really explain. It was almost like emotional overload. That is the best way I can describe it. But I could not wrap my head around any of those feelings I was having.

So, to be completely honest, I turned the attention I should have had on the Spirit to what I could see in front of me: man. My entire life I put my trust in man to find my self-worth, happiness, and love. When people were a part of my life, I put my trust in them thinking if I was a good person and treated others the way I wanted to be treated, life would be great. But I shed a lot of tears and picked up my broken pieces time after time.

Friends came and went as they tend to do over our lifetime. I put so much effort into keeping people in my life at times. Trying to make relationships work. Not wanting to let go even if I should have. I put so much time and effort into the wrong things that I spent my life struggling with my worthiness to others. And it truly comes down to putting my efforts into romantic relationships thinking that is where I would find my worth - just wanting to feel complete with that special someone. I put everything I had into these relationships for so many years. I lost myself in wanting to be with a man. Thinking that was the way life was supposed to be. I did not turn my back on God. I know that because I go back and read the journals I have written in since high school - God was there. I would ask for His help to make things good in life. But I ignored any sign He gave me telling me I was doing things wrong. My path was not supposed to be with man first, but with Him. My spiritual path was put on the back-burner for a very long time. I went thru so much heartbreak over the men who claimed to care for me and love me. I did not see what God was showing me over and over. I always believed God was there doing what He does but I did not understand. I did not realize putting my trust in man was the last thing I should be doing, but it was the only thing I had been doing. Figuring all this out took 46 years. And I did not do it alone. My journey led me to where I am right now, knowing and finding out each day what I am supposed to be doing, and sticking to the path God has put me on. With God as the forefront leading the way now, He tells me this is what I need to do. Shine the light. Pen to paper is where He gives me strength to do so. And this is where it all starts for me.

Intro

There is a progression to finding the true spirit and recognizing it for all it is. The doubts will linger for awhile because the 'not really knowing for sure definite part' is what we are seeking answers to every day. God works in mysterious ways. The timing is His. He works against another force vying for our attention. Just think about the old cartoons or even some TV shows that depict Jesus on one shoulder and Satan on the other. The battle of good and evil. Who are you going to believe and listen to? It is a daily battle we all have in some form. But those battles become fewer and fewer the more we let God's light in and shine it even brighter out. Once you open up to the job God is doing every moment of the day, let in and feel the spirit, see positivity in everything, life changes. New doors open. New feelings emerge. The light grows as all the darkness fades. Life will never be perfect, but walking with God in His spirit, it will be better, promising and brighter. More than we ever imagined.

The following pages show the way I found all this out. Long talks with God and my friend, Jeremy, lead me to put my feelings and thoughts on paper. It is my journey that started months ago when Jeremy and I became friends. He opened my eyes to things I had been missing in my life. Then, he encouraged me to write about it all when I shared a part of my journal entries with him. And now, I want to share it with you.

The God Job is something Jeremy wrote many years ago. The first time he shared it with me I was amazed by his words. I reference it a few times in the following pages. It has helped and led me to find my true spiritual side. Jeremy is very special and has so much to share. This is just the beginning for him too.

THE GOD JOB

By Jeremy Thomas

I will gain more understanding when I realize…divine action is always working on my behalf.

It's a God Job! There are simply some things in life you are not going to be able to do anything about. There will be those occasions when you simply cannot change what happens or how it happens. There will be those times in your life when your hands are tied, your mind is blank, your mouth is shut and you feel totally helpless. These are God Jobs! These are experiences of God working on you, in you, through you and for you. Although you want to get involved, although you feel the need to do something, when God is working, your job is to be still.

There is nothing more challenging than sitting through a God Job! Yes, you will feel weak. Yes, you will feel stupid. Unfortunately, there is nothing you can do nor is there anything you need to do except wait. In the midst of a God Job, there is nothing you need to say. There is no place you need to go. There is no amount of fixing, figuring out or trying that will make what you want to happen happen the way you want it to happen. When God is on the job, working on you, in and for you, there is no one and nothing on the planet that can help you through what you are going through.

In the God Job, the only course of action is total, undaunted, microscopic trust. You must become a child again. You must trust that you will be fed, that you will be changed, that you will be protected, that every need you have will be met. It may feel like you are being passive, but the truth is, if you can trust in the midst of a challenge, God can do more for you in five minutes than you can ever do in five years.

Until today, you may have been trying to do for yourself what God is on the job doing what needs to be done, working toward the best possible outcome for your best interest.

Today I am devoted to remembering that God has a plan! That's all I need to know.

And after Jeremy shared this God Job with me, I was inspired to put my journey, and every aspect of it, on paper for others to read and hopefully be inspired. And so....

THE JOURNEY BEGINS!

1

At many times in our lives, our path may feel more like a roller coaster than streams and rivers. Up and down. Bug smacks you in the face. You feel like being sick. And everything is completely out of control. There is no calm until you get to the end of the ride. If you listen to enough people over time, there will be times they describe life as being like a roller coaster because it gets out of control. Things are beyond our control. Just remember even in those times, God is always in control and will always bring you thru anything. It is only a small part of our journey. We just need to hang on. Give all our faith to God. Know and believe in the God Job. Never quit. Shine our lights no matter how many ups and downs we have to stomach, we know with our faith all is possible. Because God will always be there. And this is only one step in the journey.

2

I spend a lot of my thinking time trying to grasp life and where my path is leading me. Sometimes it feels like I am headed down a long and winding road with a blindfold on, but that is kinda what it means to walk in faith. I am trying every day to take each step forward knowing God is leading me exactly where He wants me to be. I do not want to stray from the path again. I do not want to disappoint anyone who crosses this path of mine. I know that I can do anything with the light of God shining on me. I just want to find success in what I am doing right here, right now. I want to be able to make a significant difference in my life and others by taking care of myself and them on every level: spiritually, physically, mentally, emotionally, financially, and any other way I can help each person who comes into my life. This has always been my goal. Doing all that is a challenge daily because I also have to keep myself together. I will always strive to do my best. And I am even more determined now finding my purpose and path God has led me to. Feeling so blessed because God brought a special person into my life to hold my hand as I start my journey. We are walking this together. Our faith came together at a time we both needed it. Jeremy has made me open up to the light of God being the forefront of who I want to become. This is just the beginning of something special.

3

Following the path I think I am supposed to be on can be difficult at times not knowing the true destination or how the bumps along the way will affect me. It is a daily struggle for me. Long days of self reflection and internal debates make me doubt the way I deal with the ups and downs. But turning to prayer multiple times a day has helped me get thru those daily wrestling matches within myself. The uncertainty of the outcome comes from the decisions I make and how I react to the situations I put myself in, making me question where it is all leading me. Keeping my thoughts positive and having people in my life who make me see beyond what is right in front of me has been my biggest blessing. Finding a way to bring everything I am struggling with to God has given me an outlet I ignored for a very long time. I would pray to Him, but not listen to Him. My mom always told me if I spoke to God, He would talk back to me. I took that literally. Until recently, I think I had given up that God would ever 'talk' to me. But He did. He brought me to a new place. Closer to family I needed. Placed an amazing person in my path who gave me more of a purpose than I had ever had in my life. I do not want to turn back to anything in my past. I cannot change it. It shaped me into the person I am now, so I will never regret anything I have gone thru. I intend to use it all to build something strong in myself and in my life. It is time to make a difference in the way I live life. And it is time to bring it out so others can see. It is never too late to find the path God has for you and start that journey.

4

How is it that words will bypass your brain and fall out of your mouth even as you try to think about your words before you say them? It is not always a bad thing, but it can be a negative thing you did not know was even there. This happened to me tonight while I was talking to my friend. When he pointed out what I said, the tears started to fall down my cheeks. It was not because I felt failure. And it was not because he called me out on it (that is the only way to learn). I really think the feeling I had was disappointment in myself for missing the opportunity to project positive on a negative situation. I missed the curve ball completely while I was swinging to hit that homerun in the bottom of the ninth. So, into extra innings we go. But the thing is, I am not going to hit a homerun each time I swing and we are all in a game that will only end when we leave our earthly home to arrive at our eternal one. So, until then, we must learn from the pitches we miss and when we do finally get the hit, it will not always be a homerun. Learn from each base we touch after the hit. But learn more from the ones we miss. And I am blessed with the coach who will point out to me where I went wrong and how I can do better next time. And finding my spiritual voice and higher purpose, gives me the motivation to learn from each time at bat.

5

Listening beyond a person's words is the key to understanding more than what he or she is just saying. I have always told my kids it is not always what you say that matters, it is how you say it. Good example is talking on the phone, which a lot of people don't do nowadays - especially those under the age of thirty. If you are on the phone with someone, and as you talk you are frowning or occupied by something right in front of you, the person on the other end of the phone can hear that in the way you are speaking. Just putting a smile on your face while talking can change the whole feel of what is being said. Try it! We all have had those days when the world is just not nice to us and so many things are running thru our heads and hearts. Others will pick up on that if we let it consume us and take over our entire being. If all those things are weighing us down and we cannot take care of them in the present, we need to hand them over to God. He can help with the solution we are looking for. He will take it on, releasing you to do what you need to at the moment. If you smile knowing God has your back and is in control of those things you are unable to control at the moment, your mindset changes, which will change the way you project yourself vocally, physically and mentally. The light will shine thru the cracks. And as you continue to talk to God and let Him guide you, help you, and hold you up when you need it, the cracks will get bigger, letting your light shine even more. We will always have cracks to let the light thru. Only you and the strength of your faith in what God can do will determine the size of the cracks letting your light out for others to see. And it can all start with a simple smile.

6

Going about each day, looking up, looking forward, even looking down so as not to trip on those uneven sidewalks, but trying not to look back because the past cannot be changed or re-lived in any way. Our past can be great or like a horror movie we can only watch thru our fingers as we gasp and jump. No matter what our history is - it shaped us. It gave us lessons to learn from. It gave us joy and sometimes sorrow. And in the present, it makes us think, wonder, and causes debates within ourselves. Questions will arise. Did I do it right? What could I have done differently? Why didn't I do this instead? We all have those thoughts at one time or another. The one thing we have to realize is - no matter how much we think about all that has happened, wishing we could go back and do it differently - there is no going back. That is the true undeniable reality. So while coming to terms with reality of the moment, knowing that all of that stuff you dwell on from your past won't change. But know it has shaped the person you are right now. And the way you look at and use all those memories from your past can reflect on your actions every day. The big decision you have to make is, are you going to turn those lessons into a positive or a negative. The key is to turn every negative past experience into a present positive thought. All things positive will shine your light. And your light will only get brighter.

7

Sometimes you have to let go of everything to figure out what is meant for you to hold on to. All the things in our lives we see as important might not be the things God has planned on being there for the long haul. If you are playing tug of war with your emotions over a person in your life, let go and see how God handles it for you .Give the uncertainties of not knowing over to the One who will always give you the right answer. Maybe not in the time frame you want, but that answer will come and it will be the one you need. Think of it this way: if there is a person in your life who takes and never gives, always makes you out to be the bad guy no matter the situation, does not value the person you are or trying to become, drains you on every level of your being (emotional, physical, mental, and spiritual) - just maybe it is time to loosen your grip.

8

We all have limits. No matter how strong. No matter how passionate. No matter how healthy. No matter your purpose. There will come a time you will need to take time to think about you. Your needs. Your wants. Yourself. If you don't take care of you, you cannot be effective in doing for others. We are not effective in our passion for life if we only concentrate on others. And some people do not return what you give them…attention, empathy, favors, a listening ear, and sometimes just time. You make the effort to give all these things because of who you are, but do they do that for you? No, you don't expect it. No, you don't ask for it. But you deserve it. So, take the time you need for you when you need it. It is okay. And the ones that know you will understand and let you have that time because the next time they ask, you will be right there better because you are focused and clear.

9

Not sure what my purpose is or where I am going. Most days, at some point in a twenty-four hour period, I sit and wonder about that very statement - what am I doing here. Yes, I know it is more like a question, but the weight of it in my head makes it feel like it should end with a period and not a question mark. Sounds silly. But some things are not always what they are supposed to be. Our minds and hearts don't always work together and that is why we get conflicted within ourselves. It can make life even more confusing. This is why I have difficult moments throughout my days and even more so at night. For me, alone time is not always a good thing. Lately, I have been turning to prayer more and more. I feel like it gives me a little power at a time I am powerless to all those thoughts and feelings that take over. Being able to acknowledge and turn them over to a higher power can be like a weight lifting off me. Giving me a reason to take a deep breath, refocus myself, and restore my faith in the direction I am headed. Knowing the path is there for me to follow. I just have to keep my faith in God's purpose for me above any thoughts of just not knowing. And never take for granted knowing the power God will get things done when I do not. I just need to open my eyes, take a look around me, and think about where I am; compared to where I was.

10

Life is not fair. We all know it. The cards we are dealt can be good enough to go alone and take all the tricks or maybe we need to rely on our partner to help score that point. Then, there will be times we have to pass without making trump and just play the cards in our hand trying to eucher the other team. But what it really comes down to is playing our cards to the best of our ability and have faith we score the winning point with God as our partner. We know even if the game does not go as we wanted it to, in the end with God as our partner we will always get the win. The more we focus on the end product God has in store for us and play our cards following the rules, we cannot lose even if we do not score all the points. Just remember, we will falter and the other team might get a point, but we just need to make sure we score that last point to end up on top shining with God at our side.

11

What is wrong when you get up in the morning and you don't feel too great or too bad, not negative or positive, I guess kinda indifferent is the only word that fits, but the tears start to fall. No real reason. Not really understanding myself right now. Maybe I'm scared of myself. Does that even make sense? It is not like I am going to hurt myself or anyone around me (I know that is the first thing someone would think of with that statement). There are just times I feel like I can't explain my feelings - mentally, emotionally, spiritually, or even physically. And that is why I say I'm scared. It is like I don't know why I am even here. I sit and wonder about my purpose, how I'm going to get thru the day. But at moments like this, all I can say is I don't know, but God does. Faith in the God of all things possible. He will pull me thru.

12

I am at a loss and have been for a few days. I guess when things in my life do not play out the way I think they should or I want them to, I get really down. Deep down I know I should not feel that way, but I do. I always have. Probably my biggest weakness. Then, my emotions take over and I break down. At times like this, I need to think about the God Job. Things that I am having trouble dealing with are not even in my control. How do I know this? I tell myself this. I feel like I try really hard to not let it consume me. But it does. I talk to God about it. Try really hard to hand it over to Him. But the more I try to let it all go, the more I get down about it. Then, tears will fall. At that point, I have to just let the tears fall and the emotions to flow. Bad thing is - I get totally disappointed in myself because I feel like I failed in all the things I am trying to accomplish, following God's path for me. What can I do differently? Or do I just need to keep moving forward and maybe just maybe the light will shine thru the cracks of my life.

13

It is not knowing when waking up every morning. Being thankful for just waking up and greeting a new day should be the first thought anyone has, but is that the very first thing that runs thru anyone's mind. If it is, that is amazing. Because most first thoughts of the day are:

Do I have to get up
Bathroom
Coffee
Ugggh
I'm cold
I'm hot
Is that the kids
What time is it

I could go on and on. Now, as the day gets moving, eventually the thought of gratefulness and a new day to take on new things will definitely be thought about when focus overtakes sleepy brain. No matter how hard we try or how much we want to, there is no way to focus on the positive all the time. The key is: do not give the negative power. Focus on turning the bad into good, negative to positive. Not an easy task. But just like with anything, practice daily and it gets easier. And believe it or not; it changes your outlook on each day and each moment you shine.

14

Pack up. Let's go. There is nothing left for me here. That was my mindset at the end of last year. I had been completely broken by so many things for so long not realizing what it was all doing to me on all levels of my well-being. I say my life fell apart in a three week period because that is what I believed a year ago. It is almost the one year anniversary of it all. And I'm feeling it deep down inside. I am affected. It still hurts. No matter how hard I want to suppress it all.

Coming to terms with why I am feeling this way is a battle within myself. I want to sit and get it all out, but I'm not sure I am ready to face it. There are so many things I need to face, and maybe now is the time. Time to throw it all down the way I know how - pen to paper. So here goes...

September 27th marks the one year anniversary of my best friend's sudden death. She was not sick (as far as I know) and had always been outgoing and busy. I was told she passed in her sleep, and honestly that is all I really know. It was so difficult for me to believe it happened. The only person I had for direct support at that very moment I found out was my son because he still lived at home with me. Both my kids were very close to their "aunt" Leslie. She was at the hospital the night Ryan was born. And she always made a point to be a part of my kids' lives. This made her not only my friend, but also a part of my family. She even called my parents mom and dad. So, my entire family was affected by this unexpected event. Most of them being over 800 miles away meant lots of tears over the phone. My son was my shoulder to cry on because he was right there with me.

My other best friend, Nate, tried to be there the best he could, but he was going thru his own personal troubles. Now my two best friends became friends on a night we all decided to hang out together at my house. And that just meant food, TV, laughs, and sleep. Always the simple life. We had a blast everytime we got together. (I miss all that.) But what made this time even more difficult was the boyfriend who I thought loved me had no time to help me get thru any of it. He was too busy with his newborn (not mine) and lying to me about everything. (I'll get to that.)

Losing the one person I had always been able to count on, outside my family, was almost unbearable. We didn't talk all the time. We only saw each other four or five times a year, but I could always count on Leslie. No matter what was going on, She would always be there for me. I don't feel like I was there for her the way she was for me. There are many things about Leslie's life I did not know about and it hurts that I wasn't as good a friend to her as she was to me. The reason I say that is because when her brother passed away (I believe in March) she didn't reach out to me at all. I admit, I was going thru some stuff, but I always seem to be. I feel like I wasn't a very good friend and that makes me very sad.

Writing and thinking about all this makes me feel very disappointed in myself. I always wanted to be the one that others would count on in their time of need. I did not give that to someone who meant the world to me. I thank God for all the special times we spent together and will never forget her.

A few weeks after Leslie went to be in Heaven, where I will see her again someday, the person I thought I was going to spend my life with decided he wanted to be with the mother of the child he had with her while we were together. Messed up, right? I don't know another way to explain it. I am sure you can imagine how that story goes. I was dedicated to him in every way thinking he would be dedicated to me completely one day. I should have known that the lying and cheating would never stop and should have walked away when I first found out. God tried to tell me over and over again (I know that now), but I did not want to see it, I did not listen. I believed what I wanted to, no matter how many times God waved those flags in my face. But I hung in there. I believed my boyfriend's words, but did not hold him accountable for his actions. Then, two days after my birthday, he not only broke up with me, but broke me completely. I did not know what to do. I was lost and hurt. And guess what? That is not the end of it.

My parents had come up from Texas to help my son pack and move him down there. I thought I was going to be moving in with said boyfriend and live happily ever after. That was not going to happen, but my son was sure moving 800 miles away from me. He needed to be closer to more family and pursue life. I was scared. I was going to be alone for the first time in my life. I had no clue where life was going to take me. I felt I would never get past all of this. What I did not understand was, when it feels like your life is falling apart, what is really going on is God is creating so much more for you. Everything happens for a reason. God has a plan for all of us. We do not always understand and may never understand, but His plans for us are bigger than we can even imagine. When you think your world is falling apart, maybe it is more like your world is falling into place. And for my situation, that is exactly what was happening. Trust in the process no matter what it is, God knows what we need and when we need it in all situations.

15

Good things are happening. With lots of patience and positive vibes, I feel God blessing me every day. He still is doing "the job" in His time, and it is the *only* way. To be honest, the challenges of Satan still hit me at odd angles and I can recognize them quicker, but catch myself at times lifting my foot to move backward instead of forward. That is when I just have to stop (everything). Regroup. Then, push myself forward. There have been a few times my foot landed on the ground behind me. Disappointed in myself. The prayers start. Asking for forgiveness. Wisdom. Strength to push myself forward and not repeat my faltered step. I am very thankful that I have a person who came into my life to help me with my journey and the enlightenment I have been searching for my whole life without totally realizing it. My focus has never been on that aspect of my being. It took over 46 years and the right person engaging that side of me to make it my reality. Everything happens for a reason and when it is supposed to happen. I truly believe that more and more every day. It took me falling apart completely to be able to rebuild myself better with the support and guidance God put in my path to find my true light and purpose.

16

Life can change so quickly even when it feels like time moves slowly some days. It does not seem like almost a year since life threw me my second biggest curve ball. I've had many curves thrown at me in my life as we all have, but losing Leslie was one I didn't see coming. Then again, no one saw Leslie leaving us so early. But sometimes, God decides He needs that special angel now. He had a job to be done that no one else could do. Leslie was unique and just had a way about her. She is fulfilling her purpose from above us. No doubt in my mind about that. She was special to me in so many ways for so many years. It is still hard for me to really believe I will never see her again (on earth). Of course, I know we will meet again. But I miss the fun of just hanging out and laughing. For the most part, our friendship was simple and holds so many memories. We had some ups and downs, but I always knew I could count on her. And I hope she felt the same way about me. I miss my friend! But she is in the best place ever and I will join her when it is my time.

17

Every person's journey is different. How and why it starts. When it starts. Technically our journey of life starts the moment we enter the world. But I feel our spiritual journey is a little different. It can be like driving. Sometimes it is stop and go. At times, it might be all highway. Of course, we all make wrong turns or get completely lost sometimes. There is a lot of defensive driving that keeps you aware of your surroundings and the people who cannot follow the traffic laws. In Indiana, it was about avoiding potholes. In Texas, it has been more about bad drivers changing three lanes at a time. But the whole time you are behind the wheel, you are in control of how you drive. Where your focus is. And how you react to the chaos all around you. The same is true for your spiritual journey. And just remember, sometimes you are a passenger taking your journey with someone special. Working together to reach that destination meant for you. Take your journey.

18

I never know how the words are going to come out. Writing has always been the way I process my feelings, my life, and now my spiritual journey. Verbal can be easy to some degree, but writing has always been my biggest strength. We all have ways to deal with life. Finding peace and happiness in this world of chaos is the biggest challenge we all face. It has to start within. Looking inside ourselves is a very difficult and will be lifelong process. We constantly work to find peace and happiness. The key to making life work in your favor is never to quit on yourself. Go after what you deserve. Keep focus. But never forget, whatever it is we are striving for, we are only in control of ourselves. And that is not enough to make it in this world. But when it comes down to it all, we need a little help. God is going to provide a way for us to reach the place we are meant to be. Earthly needs and wants will always be a part of life, but just know God is the one who leads us and guides us to our greater purpose which is the light of our destiny. The light God will shine on us and thru us, making the way on our path to more. It just takes faith in knowing God will lead us to amazing things and the purpose we are meant to fulfill.

19

Some days it all comes so easy. My focus is good. My thoughts have all smiley faces on them. My actions and reactions are spot on for the world to say 'look at that' and remember all the good God does. I want every day to be just like that. But no matter how hard we try, we have to remember Satan is working just as hard as God. He is determined to sway us away from God. When we realize that is what is happening, we are more likely to change the way we deal with the times we are just not feeling it. The 'it' I am referring to is our inner light God provides us to shine. This is when we need to take the time to reflect and know God is there waiting for us. What is He waiting for you to ask? God waits for us to remember:

> He is ALWAYS there
> He is our BFF
> He will provide
> He loves us (no matter what)
> All we have to do is have true faith
> In all He can do
> PERIOD!

20

There will be days where you do everything you are supposed to do, the way you are supposed to do it, thinking nothing can go wrong. The day is good. Then, something happens and your good vibes and positive thoughts explode right in front of you. The tears start to come. You feel you have no control over anything, especially the overflowing of emotion. So, what do you do? Deep down you know everything you should be doing and where your mind should be. It is all in God's time. Everything happens for a reason, even when we don't know what it is. Have faith in God and His plan. Personally, I try to remember the God Job. Then, I call my friend and ultimately my spiritual therapist. I have this talk with him. Tell him how I feel, how my head is telling me to do all the things I know I'm supposed to, but not being able to put it into action. He prays for me (as he has done many times) which makes me cry a little more. But after our conversation and a little more casual chatting, we said we would talk later. At that point, I took some time to really think about all I said and he said to me. I had to really sit and process all of it. Once I took time to put it all into perspective, I felt a kind of calm take over. Nothing was fixed. Nothing was really different other than the way I felt. I think sometimes, we just need to hear a voice of reason out loud to overpower the voice of destruction in our heads.

21

Not knowing is the hardest part of life. But can also be the most exciting too. We don't ever know for sure what will happen minute to minute. We plan. We execute. And results happen. But there is no plan we make, attempt to execute exactly like we plan, and see the exact results we want. There is no such thing as perfection in life on this earth. The only thing we can do to get things done is try our hardest and ask God for guidance. With His guidance, we can achieve anything as long as we have true faith. Believe in His plans for us. His outcome might not be what we expect or want, but we must be patient to where it all leads. What we consider a failure, God may see as a success because it will lead to the bigger things He has planned for us. Sometimes a bad outcome can open the door to an amazing opportunity we never saw coming. But God knew. God has a plan. God is always working. And we won't always see it. We just have to have faith in God's job, making our job to trust, keep moving forward, and never give up on what He is doing in our lives.

22

Looking for my light today. The purpose of what God is leading me to do. The path has turned into a mountain before me. Time to take a deep breath and start climbing. As I look up at the challenge, I know it is time for a pep talk. God always listens. So, I take it directly to Him. Not only my concerns and worries, but also my blessings and gifts. They are what linger in my mind. Even my heart feels a little heavy right now. God will take on the weight I feel, so I can rise up to fulfill my purpose of the day every day. I just have to remember daily that it is not about me. It is about the purpose of my words and actions. To light the way for myself and all the people I can touch and inspire. So they see what He is doing in my life and can do it in theirs. Finding my calling. Finding my purpose. Finding my truth. Discovering what I am supposed to be doing and making my journey the best it can be.

23

The more I think about where I am going, the clearer I become. It is not about me, nor has it ever been. It is about what I do, what I can do, and what I will do. The purpose of why I am here. The visions I am creating in my head. The words I can put on paper. The feeling I spread to others. It all makes me who I am supposed to be. It is not the same for everyone. Timing is going to be different. What is meant for each person is different. We are not the same for a reason. Which means our purpose in life cannot be the same as others. And the way we fulfill our purpose depends on how we use the tools God puts in our path.

24

Talking to my friend Jeremy today, a picture popped into my head. I do not think anything like that had happened to me before, at least not in the positive sense. It was not a dream. It was what I would describe as a true vision. It went like this:

Jeremy - my friend
Standing in a field
About 3 feet of empty field around him
Outside that 3 feet are people covering the rest of the field
As far as the eye could see
Jeremy was not on a stage
Or a mountain
Or even a pedestal
He was just standing on the ground
And the people all around
Were just waiting

My thought is Jeremy has a purpose to lead people with his words and testimonies. People are going to listen. His words and passion are going to touch people in a way no one else ever has. Jeremy is special. God is working thru him. And the thing is, God picked the right person for this job. Jeremy has a way with how he expresses the words God is giving him. He helped me find my path, my purpose and start my journey. I will forever be grateful for him coming into my life. He makes me smile. He makes me think. He challenges me like no one ever has. He gives me support and encouragement like I have never experienced before. It is so difficult to put into words all the feelings I have for this man. He is my inspiration to shine my light.

25

Woke up thinking this morning. Big topic:

Unanswered Prayers

We are always told to take it all to God. Say your prayers. God is always listening. But in my case, I think I always got upset when I would pray for something specific and it would not happen the way I prayed for it. Then, I would remember my mom telling me that God answers all prayers in His time, not ours. So, I would continue to pray thinking I just needed to wait and God would surely give me what I wanted if I just kept asking. *So not true.* This all reminded me of a song, "Unanswered Prayers" sung by Garth Brooks. I felt it every time I heard it. I understood it. But I did not take time to really apply it to my life until now. The point of the song is: God answers all our prayers in some way - maybe not exactly how we want Him to though. For example, many times I have asked for happiness or even peace of mind. Usually, I was referring to the relationship I was in at the time. So something would happen (red flag) that would cause the opposite effect of what I prayed God to do. I might find out I'm being cheated on again. Definitely not a happy thing nor did it give my mind any peace. But God was showing me the red flags to open my eyes and take action. He knew I would be happier and deserved better without that person in my life. But of course, I did not catch what He was throwing right at my face. I was unhappy for a very long time. This was a repeating pattern. It took until now to really understand that unanswered prayers are a blessing because God has a plan and He is always on the job.

26

Turning up the music. Just get lost in the words. Feel the lyrics.

This is what I did tonight because I was having thoughts I could not control. And when asked by a friend what was wrong, I did not want to vocalize them. I have been trying so hard not to say certain things out loud because it gives them power. My friend and I have talked about this often. Because I knew all the stuff going on in my head was negative, I did not want to give all th\ose things more power than what they already had over me. But he got me to spill part of it. I cried because I felt guilty for having all those negative thoughts about myself and a certain situation I am in right now. I have spent the past couple of days praying about it, but sometimes I feel like I'm not saying the right words in my prayers. I try to tell myself even if the words are not quite right, God knows my heart. I have to have faith He really understands the person I am and the person I am trying to be. I have to put my mind at ease by telling myself that no matter what God knows I'm trying. And as I sit and listen to the uplifting lyrics of my favorite contemporary Christian music, my heart lights up and my mind starts to ease. Of course, talking to my friend always helps too. Music has always had a huge impact on my mood and thoughts at difficult times. I just have to remember not to give my thoughts power at times like this. It is a process I am working on every day.

27

Words have more meaning than any of us realize. And it is not just what is said but how it is said. It really can be just that simple.

28

Restoring my mind and my emotions is a challenge on my bad days. But I work on myself daily. Positive thoughts from the negative feelings. Finding my happy place. Sometimes the closet is best. And all that means is having those private conversations with God and no one else. That is going to my closet.

29

Looking to a Higher Power to take over all the things in your life that you are unable to control is a difficult concept to grasp. Faith in something you cannot physically see in front of your face daily is even more difficult to wrap your head (and heart) around. But when you think about it, we see people all day long. Right? Think about all those times we have put faith in a person and got let down, hurt, and sometimes even crushed. Then, you might think of the times you felt God did not answer your prayers. We have all had these thoughts. But have you ever thought that God did answer those prayers. Maybe not in the way you wanted or in the time frame you expected, but believe it or not He did answer them according to the plan, path and journey He wants you to take. Think about it. Then, take a minute to think about the prayers you may not have prayed directly to Him, but He is always there, always working, knows you better than you know yourself. He answered without you even asking. God is never-ending and so is His love and patience for all who have faith in what He can do and will do. Just look at what He does every day for us. Take a minute to look around you and just see. Faith in God not man.

30

Thinking about the wonders around us. The sun, moon, mountains, animals, flowers, and so many more for us to be thankful for every day. What we don't really think about most days is where all these things come from. Life is busy. We all lose sight of the simplicity of life. We expect so much out of ourselves and others. We get lost in our big expectations for more. The thing we need to remember is with true faith in all God can do, all our needs will be provided for. We just need to open our eyes and hearts to the simple things in life. God will provide the opportunities for us. Thru our conversations and our private thoughts we share with God, He knows everything we just want even if it is not necessary to live. All the things God will do for us and even thru us, will be for reasons we may not understand, but have to trust Him. The more trust we have, the more faith we show, the more at peace we will feel at times when all seems impossible and out of control. So, hand it over to God and have trust and true faith in what happens next.

31

Waking up in the morning and being thankful for another day should be easy. Thanking God for opportunities to touch someone with a kind word or smile, more time to spend with people we love, another chance to reach our goals, or even just to have more chances to shine the light God has given to you. It is amazing if you get up in the morning and those are your first thoughts. The day will shine thru the rain. I have tested it. Guess what? It works. There is always going to be something or someone throughout your day that will try to take away the positive mindset you are trying to achieve. Rise up above the negative that crosses your path, especially the negative that enters your mind. Change it all into a positive. The more you do it the easier it gets. I challenge you.

32

True inspiration comes from within. We may get inspired by outside sources or events but it is all about how we process those things that go on around us. It can even develop by the way other people react to what is going on. We can feel the vibrations of situations we are in and people we are around if we are completely open to it. Think about it this way, the Gibbs' gut. If you have watched NCIS you understand the reference. It is the feeling we get when we know, but can't explain. Then, we must get the evidence to prove. And that is all about our testimonies.

33

Today something is telling me I have a higher purpose that I have yet to truly discover. What I can say to that is…dreams of what I wanted to do in my life are still lingering out there in the universe. I have always tried to do my best. I have not always made the right decisions. Even at 46 years old, I am still messing up. To be completely honest, day to day I do not know what I am doing. I have been trying very hard to take a step forward every day, talk to God (even though I never know for sure I am saying anything the right way), look for the positive in everything and everyone who crosses my path, and soul searching for my true purpose in life. I question my abilities. I question who I am. More directly, who God wants me to be. I have questions and doubts that I cannot carry and expect to move forward physically, mentally, emotionally; or most important to me right now, spiritually. So, every day I say a prayer and let God know where I am lacking, asking only for His guidance to lead me where He wants me to go. I want to be an inspiration to others, but I lack finding my own inspiration some days. I get in my head how I want to do things to move forward in my journey of finding my purpose and making things happen, but the next moment I get lost. I am unable to figure out how to put it all together and shine the light. How do I get myself to focus on how to just make it happen? All I can do right now is to continue to ask the Good Lord to provide me with a little beam of light to show me what I am supposed to be doing. It does not have to be anything like the bat signal, but a little ray of light would help me figure it out…

34

Dear God,

I do not know what I am doing. I try to be patient and let things happen the way they are supposed to. I know You have a plan. I know You are in control. I know You are on the job every day. I want what is best for everyone. I just cannot figure out if I am doing it right. I honestly do not know if I am doing what You want me to do. I am really trying. But some days I get really down. Not sure why. So, I guess what I am saying is I need You to help me, to lead me where I am supposed to be going, show me what I am supposed to be doing. I want my faith in all You do to be so much greater than my fear of myself and facing each day. I know I need to get a handle on myself. I am looking for a way to do just that. I feel like I don't know anything some days. I need your help to find myself and for You to lead me. I know I can't hide anything from You. So, You know where I am. I cannot fall apart again. Please help me!

35

No matter how hard we try- no matter how much time we spend planning - no matter how much we pray - no matter how strong our faith - *nothing is ever going to be perfect* (on earth)! There are too many factors that play into everything we do or try to do. We only have so much control. What we have to remember is God has the ultimate control. Timing is everything. And it is not our timing. It's about God's timing. God's true plan for us individually and together is where His focus is. We need to have faith in God's plan and the path He has us on. He will make sure we are taken care of. That does not mean we let Him do everything. We have to put in effort. We have to do our part. When we don't know what that is, we have to ask for guidance and focus to stay on the path laid before us to continue our journey forward. When we don't get things in the order or time we think we should, just remember it is not about us. It is about God's plan for us, and He is always on the job!

36

So many times during the day, I look up just wondering where I am really headed in life. Ultimately, in my heart, I know where I want to go, things I want to do, people I want to be around, and the difference I want to make in the world. Then, it is time to talk to God about it. I want to make sure I am doing what God wants me to do. It is important for me right now to know if I am on the right path, following the direction He is leading me. Sometimes the thing I can say to God is, "You know what is in my heart and in my mind. Please lead me where I am supposed to go." All I want to do is what He has planned for me. There are many times my faith does not feel strong enough. I just have to keep working on that while God is working on me. I just want to be the best version of myself for all those I love. As my best friend Jeremy would say, "Shine your light." Every time he tells me that I think to myself, "How do I really do that?" All I can do is move forward a step at a time. Listen for God's directions. Take action. And that is exactly what I will do.

37

~~~~~~~~~~~~~~~~~

The very moment Jeremy started talking to me about getting his testimonies on paper and presented to the world, I was hooked. The idea that I could finally write the book I had always wanted to, but could never find the inspiration. Jeremy gave me something I had never had before, a true purpose. He brought out something different in me. Made me see things differently. Helped me dig deep into things I had not thought of in a very long time. Gave me a different kind of hope and faith. Lifted me in a way no one ever had before. Jeremy gave me a reason. Since all our talks started, I have written more and in a different way. My mindset is clearer. It is lighter. Jeremy coming into my life has been the biggest blessing. God knew what I needed, who I needed and when I needed it. I believe this project will say more than anyone realizes. I have not mentioned it to too many people because I want it to be an amazing surprise for everyone. It is definitely my saving grace.

38

When you wake up and the first thing on your mind is 'how is today going to be great,' you know deep down life is good. God has blessed you with a new outlook on life, given you a light to see as soon as you open your eyes. Having the first thought, when you wake up, being positive will change your whole day. Personally, I know what that is like. Monday morning means the start of a new work week at a job you have to do because we all have bills to pay, food to buy, and all that other stuff which takes money to live. And truth be told, many people out there do not like or enjoy the job they 'have to' go to every day. Now, there are many reasons not to like a job, but ultimately I feel like a lot of people don't have passion for what it is they are doing. There are many reasons we are not passionate about things we do - work or otherwise. Sometimes when the passion for something is not initially there, we may just need to create it. Wondering how to make that happen? Positivity! Find the positive in everything you do, in every person you encounter, and especially in every thought that passes thru your head. I know it sounds like an impossible task to do, but remember what all those teachers, coaches and even your parents told you growing up, "practice makes perfect." Yes, I know there is no such thing as perfect (unless you are speaking of God), but the more you do something the easier it gets. It will become your normal. There is not one thing you do in your life right now that was easy the first time you did it, but it *got easier* the more you did it. It is all one day at a time, moving forward with positive words and actions whenever something negative steps into your path. And remember, everything negative is Satan's work to keep us away from God's work. Every time we conquer negative with positive Satan loses power and God gains it. Only good can come from that, right?!

39

HARRY POTTER - DUMBLEDORE'S PENSIEVE

While having a talk with my son about thoughts of things or people that overpower anything else in your brain, I started thinking about the pensive Dumbledore uses in the Harry Potter series. Can't remember which book (or movie) it was introduced in, but I believe it has significant meaning in our daily lives. Let me explain. We all have many things that run thru our minds every second of the day. Could be stuff we need to remember and some we don't. They might not be negative or positive but they are taking up space and time. It is more than likely thoughts of things we have no control over. For my son, it was about a girl. Not good or bad, just thoughts taking up space when his focus needed to be elsewhere. And he told me he did not know how to get those thoughts to go away or be put on the backburner so he could focus on what he needed to do right now. That is when I thought about putting those unnecessary thoughts away until we wanted to deal with them. That is exactly what I used my journaling for over years. I would write things down and put my thoughts away. It helped me get rid of the negative in my head that I could not deal with at that time in life. What I'm saying is when you have things overpowering your head, it makes it difficult to focus on the positive. So, let go of all those things in your head (and heart) that you have no control over to make room for the positive you do have control of. Write it down. Put it away/ We don't have a pensive but we can find out what works for us individually. Make room for the things that feel good, make us smile, gives us opportunities to shine and help others feel the vibrations to focus on the *awesomeness* God shows us daily.

40

⚜

Stuff

Many people in the world will base a person's worth on what he has or does not have. Deep down I never understood that because stuff is just stuff. Easy come, easy go. And sometimes hard to get, but still easy to go. I have always looked at a person for who they were, or I guess what they appear to be. For some reason, I could look beyond stuff, but would fall for words. I have never looked at what a person has and thought I want that person to be a part of my life. Car, house, newest technology, expensive furniture, going out all the time, lots of time on vacations, or just anything to spend money on. Don't get me wrong, having money and stuff is nice, but it is not who a person is. And that is what I focus on. Really getting to know who someone is takes time. People hide who they really are. And a lot of times, they will hide behind the stuff they have or focus on how they can get more. But then again, they will also hide behind words and tell you what you want to hear. Stuff you can see, words are more difficult to find the truth. This is when seeking God will help us find the truth in any person we come into contact with. We are supposed to love every single person because that is what Jesus tells us to do. Not easy. But we should be able to show everyone empathy and compassion without losing our ability to not get lost in stuff or false words. God has given us all free will. And that is where we have the ability to follow Him and shine by seeking the truth in others and helping those who need to find the same exact thing. Stuff does not matter. Words do matter. Actions reveal who we are. We need to keep all those things in mind always.

41

How do you know you are on the right path, doing the right things, and serving your true purpose? Honestly, I do not have the answer to that very important series of questions. And I am sure the answer is not the same for each person. But just maybe there are multiple answers for each person. Some people will say God talks to them in some way. Some people will say they feel God's presence in everything. Some might even tell you they have not received any kind of confirmation from God, but will continue doing what they do. We all have some form of direct line to God. We can talk to Him anytime. He listens to us even when we do not talk directly to Him. God knows us. He always knows more than anyone else knows about us. God is our own personal cheering section. Sometimes we forget. Sometimes we do not recognize when God is 'speaking' to us. Just because we have a direct line to Him does not mean He uses a direct line back to us. We need to be open and aware of the many different ways God 'speaks' to us.

42

When will I know? I feel lost at times because I just really do not know if I am doing all this right. Of course, I would like to think I am. I do my best, but can I do better? I believe the answer to that is, we can always do better. There is no such thing as perfect on earth. We can strive for it. We should strive for it, even though we will not reach it until our journey takes us thru those 'pearly gates' and we meet our Maker. At that very moment, perfection is all we see. Until then we must keep going, do the right things, and strive for everything good.

43

Looking around. Seeing what is in front of me. Taking it all in. Living in the moment. Wanting to know where it is all leading. Only knowing God's light is shining on me from every direction. I hold my hand out needing it to be held just to feel real. Finding inspiration in all those around me.

44

❧⟶❧

Saying "I love u"

We should love everyone. God tells us that and it should be what we feel all the time. Of course, being human, we have many feelings. Sometimes our feelings are difficult to explain to others, and at times to ourselves. We will feel mixed emotions because of all the outside factors that weigh on us. When our feelings or emotions are challenged, we have to remember that is one thing we have control over. We should absolutely love and accept people for who they are, friends, family, acquaintances, everyone. We may not always agree. We may not really like the person's words or actions, but we can show every single person love. God did. And when He did, they changed. Think about that. Showing one person love who may not know love could change their life and yours. That is the type of love we have control over.

Now, the love we do not have control over would be who we "fall in love with." There are many reasons we may fall in love with someone and sometimes it lasts, other times it does not. And that kind of love has many factors. When you find "the one", it is easy to focus on the physical because that is the first instinct, mental and emotional may be a little more challenging because it is about words and actions. Those three categories are easily manipulated. Think about it…I don't think I need to make a list. If you take a minute to think about how a person can fool you physically, mentally and emotionally, you might just surprise yourself. Because man or woman is easily manipulated by Satan when allowed, these are the areas he will use to confuse us. With God as our spiritual guide, the spirituality of our being is where the true colors shine. You start talking about the grace of God and the part He plays in your life, the love you have for someone can change. You will feel something different for that person when it starts with the three basics. It is the fourth that could lead you to something more real than you even imagined. It will not be instantaneous because really awesome things happen over time. It will be over time when you have those long in depth conversations, when you realize God put this very special person in your path for a good reason, when you want more for them and will give anything you have to make it happen, when that person has the very same ideas and thoughts on the important aspects of life. Then, you say your prayers thanking God for the path He put you on that led you to this amazing person you never want to lose.

45

It has been brought to my attention that I may be doing it wrong. And I had no clue. It kind of reminds me of the movie Mr. Mom. When Daddy had to take over all the stuff Mommy did for years, he does things the way he thinks he should and everyone is telling him he is doing it wrong. Well, no one ever showed him how to do it, so he was just winging it. Then, someone points out 'you're doing it wrong'. He got frustrated. Hit rock bottom before finding his own way to do things 'the right way, his way.' I feel like Mr. Mom did. Trying to find a way to do things the right way but also with my own twist. Right now, what I am trying to figure out is, the right way to pray and talk to God. This is really not something that is taught to you by anyone, at least not in detail. It is kind of something you do by watching and listening to others. I was educated on prayer today, and I have been doing it wrong. Jeremy told me once you take a worry or concern to God asking for help or guidance, there is no need to keep asking over and over again for the same thing. Because once we hand something to God, it is our job to have faith in what God can do (The God Job). We just need to wait. He hears what we say. And He is working to get things done. All we have to do is have faith. Sometimes that is not easy for us. But believing God is on the job, He only wants what is best for us, and all He asks from us is to have faith. Should be simple. But we must keep in mind - His time - His way. The answers we get may not be the outcome we were looking for but each day opens a new door. And just know one ending leads to a new beginning. One example I can give you about that is, when my life was in a downward spiral, I prayed for God to let me know what to do. The answer did not come right away. It was not even the answer I wanted. But I knew it was what God wanted me to do. My uncle offered me a place to live, a job, and to flip and sell my house, all I had to do was pack up my life and move. I knew I had too. I knew it was the answer God was giving me. It was not the answer I wanted or was looking for, but I just knew it was what I needed. God was telling me I needed to get out of my situation and start fresh. I am so glad I listened and did not ignore Him hoping for the answer I really wanted. Remember, we may not understand until we have faith. And I just had faith God was leading me to better. And He did.

46

Learning more and more each day that the Good Lord will always provide. Faith is everything. It does not cost us anything. But it is worth the most. We are blessed in different ways. Hidden blessings are probably the most important and the most difficult to understand. When you accept God into your heart and start to walk in faith, everything that goes on in your life, God has His hands on you. Even when you mess up - especially when you mess up. He made you in His image and wants you to follow the path He has placed right in front of you. When you stray, He will not give up on you. God has more patience with you than you can even fathom. He won't give up. He is always willing to listen. He will always forgive. God will not bring up your past and throw it in your face. When He forgives, He forgets as long as you walk in faith. He will cry with you in tough times. He will celebrate the victories. He will never give up on you.

47

God works in mysterious ways. It happens in His time. He is always on the job. God will always provide in our time of need and all we have to do is have faith in His abilities. Always be on the lookout for the ways God is working in our lives. It is not obvious in our eyes most days (and nights). This is why we must keep an open mind even thru the most difficult times. That is when we are tested the most by Satan. And that is when God is working His hardest and we have to have the most faith. The answers we get from God will not always be the ones we want. We must realize our ideas of where we want to go are not always the same as God's planned path for us. And that is where we must be the most aware of when He is 'speaking' to us, thru us, and within us.

48

So what happens when you get hurt and do not take measures to let your body heal properly, God gives you a wake up call that you have to pay attention to. That is a testimony my friend Jeramy gave me tonight. And he made it make sense. The thing is, he hurt his hand almost two weeks ago. I took him to the hospital to have it looked at even though he didn't want to. Because Jeremy did not do things to keep his hand safe so it would heal, he had another hand accident so he would have to pay attention to giving his hand the proper care it needs. He took something most people would look at as a negative and turned it into a positive sign from God. He is being taught it is time to take care of things he needs to do for himself so he can be more for others. Makes sense to me. Jeremy has so much to offer the world. He loves everyone and is the most positive person I have ever met, but he is not taking care of himself. He has been through so much which makes him amazing for wanting to share everything he has with the world. But what Jeremy has to realize, he needs to be whole to share all he has with everyone else. That is true for everyone.

49

I am not sure what I want. I am not sure what I am doing. I am not sure where I am going. I do know I want more. I do know I want a true purpose. I do know I want to be happy on every level of my being. But how do I get there? How do I make that all happen? The only real answer I can come up with is God, prayers, and faith. That is the answer to all questions we do not have answers to. After that, it is patience. So, take a huge deep breath and just know.

50

Why do I feel like I am falling behind? Do I expect too much? Is my patience lacking at the moment? Am I afraid of things not going my way? Feeling confused at the moment. And I know Satan is making me question all of these things just to throw me off my path, taking my time away. It is my time to shine and take the next step. Satan has infringed on my peace for long enough. I have a purpose. We all do. Satan wants us to doubt that purpose so we stray away from God. Satan wants control over us. We have to keep our feet on the right path knowing God will lead us to better and provide all we ever need. I will stay on the path. I will trust God to lead me to my greater purpose. I will not let Satan change my path. I will keep praying and listening to the answers God is providing. Positive, not negative. Hopeful, not fearful. Patient, not hurried. Peace, not war (within myself).

I just can't give up because I know that there is a reason and God is on the job.

51

God is in control, but Satan does things in our lives to lead us away from God. It is all very confusing. I won't deny that at all. Satan wants us to be confused. It makes us easy targets. When we start questioning if God is on the job, Satan is working on our weakness of doubting God's love for us. At one time or another, we have strayed from where God was leading us because Satan flashed a bright light that caught our attention. But that is a flash of light and not the continuous light God shines. We cannot make Satan's flash distract us from the true, lasting shine God showers over us.

52

I just had the most amazing conversation with the person I will call my spiritual and emotional therapist. My whole life I have been trying so hard to fix everything for everyone. I felt it was my job to do everything I could to make others happy and make things as easy as possible for those around me. I never tried to make anything about myself. Well, thru an enlightening discussion I learned I was doing it wrong.

53

Being blessed and thankful are the best feelings to have every day, but at times the most difficult to recognize. There are times we may have to dig deep to find the good just because the blanket of darkness and negativity is so heavy on us. And when we feel too weak to get out from under the pressure Satan adds; we must ask the Good Lord for strength to reach the light. If we ask, He will listen. Then, we need to open up for the answer. Be ready. Be cautious of Satan throwing an answer out also. The more faith we have in God's answers, the easier it will be to know when Satan is trying to trick us. Not easy. We will all make mistakes. But the more we practice tuning into God's ways and the job He is doing (on us, thru us, for us), the light will shine on our true direction staying on this path. It is there. We will feel it more intense as we grow in the spirit of God's love for us and the purpose He wants us to fulfill. It is all about living in the light and overcoming the darkness which is forced in our lives wanting to dim the light. That is when we need to shine the brightest. Focusing on our true purpose and following the path God put before us will do that with ease.

54

Positive vibes to start the day. No matter what, no negative force will invade my space. Feeling thankful for another day. Light is on. Darkness falls away. Going to find my way. On the path before me. Staying between the lines. Not to cross even a toe to the other side, as I focus on my purpose. Shine bright with a smile. All words of encouragement. To help all others see. God is here. Always doing His job. In the most unexpected ways. Thru the most unexpected means.

55

My closet. Not in the physical or literal sense. But my internal quiet place to talk to God and reflect on how all things can be a true blessing in my life. I was introduced to this special place by the amazing person who came into my life at just the right time. He let me know whenever we are unsure about *anything*, we need to take it to our closet and pray on it. Have that mental conversation with God. When we do that, Satan is unable to take it and twist it to make us doubt. Our words when spoken or even put on paper give them power. And it can either be positive with light or negative with darkness. It is our choice.

56

Jesus walks among us in some form. The time is coming where we will not have anywhere to hide. All the things in your life you use to cover your true self will fall away. So when that happens, how big of a pile will you have to climb over to get to the Promised Land? Maybe it is time to shed all those layers now.

57

I know you cannot continue to do the same things the same way and expect a different outcome. Relationships, jobs, even getting up in the morning. Actions and attitude are two things that need to be looked at when searching for a different result to a situation. And these are the two things others can see and recognize change in. Walking around with your shoulders sagging to the floor and a frown on your face is a demonstration of defeat which will make you feel bad physically, mentally and emotionally keeping people from approaching you. This action will keep you from meeting a new friend, seeing an amazing sunset, or finding opportunity in the world you have been praying for. Prayer is not the only thing we need to get a positive outcome in our lives. We have to do our part while God does His. We have to project what we are looking for in return.

58

The words I keep hearing even when they are not being spoken to me are "Shine your light." And I keep trying to figure out how to do that. I know I can do anything if I set my mind to do it and even more so with God's guidance. But there is something else that makes it more to me right now. That is having a friend to make it all happen. Having the same vision, giving and getting encouragement on the daily. That is something I have never had my whole life. Now, don't get me wrong, I have a great family and my upbringing was as good as they come. I was always set on making my parents proud of me. Doing well in school and playing sports. But I really messed up a few times. They never gave up on me though. I think I messed a few things up, not because it wasn't there the whole time, but because my focus was different. The people in my life had the same type of focus I did. I am not saying that the Spirit did not have a place in our lives, it is just we kept the light on the lowest setting. Can't say why. But looking back, that is what is coming to mind. It took a person with the right words, the right mindset at just the right time to bring me out of my darkness, from under my blanket of Satan's words and actions in my life to find the lit path God has put before me to lead me to my purpose. And my purpose is right here. The power of words followed by the actions I take to make those words reality has become my focus.. Some days it is not easy. Satan is always watching, listening, and scheming to put that blanket over me again. I may falter at times, as we all will, but our faith in God and His ultimate power when open to it, we can all find the light to shine in our words and all we do. It is there. God is always there. Satan is too, but the more we shine the light, the love, and the reason, the less power Satan has in our lives and those we touch, inspire, and encourage.

59

Don't Sweat the Small Stuff...we have all heard it. We have all probably put some thought into it. Some of us may have the book. But what is the small stuff? According to my friend: *everything*! When you have complete faith in God, it is all small stuff because He can get us thru anything that is put in our path. Nothing in our lives is really permanent if you think about it. Only our faith in what God does, has done and will do is a permanent fixture in our lives every day. That is one thing we can stand behind, stand up for, and stand our ground when it comes to our faith. As long as we do our part, God will do His. The guarantee no one can deny.

60

Today Angel 17 is telling me I am on the right path headed for great things. Everything is in motion. On a day like today, this is just what I need to hear (or read). Getting introduced to Angel numbers has been very helpful to me. When I look one up, it makes me feel like this is God speaking to me in a way He knows I will get it. And most days that is just what I need. It gives me a renewed calm and focus in my head and even more in my heart. At a time where I feel confused and unsure in many moments of the day, knowing where I can turn to for a little boost or kick-in-the-butt is exactly what I need. God knows that. I believe He is helping push me along my path a little quicker right now. Gotta get it done.

61

Signs…they are everywhere. Tesla even had a really cool song about the way signs are worded and how people react to them. (Yes, I know it was a cover song, but it is the version I enjoy.) We can all read physical signs right in front of us that are printed. We can think about them (or not), analyze them, interpret them, and come to a conclusion as to what signs are trying to convey. But what about the ones that are difficult to see, because they are not written and plastered in front of us. Signs are given to us every single day by way of words, actions, and events. The ones we have to really think about in a certain moment in time and maybe those are the signs that have the most meaning. Sometimes it can be a preview to something the future has in store for us. How can we tell? Honestly, I have absolutely no clue. And I am not sure anyone has that true insight just 'to know.' We must pray for God to reveal it all to us. And He will. As long as we have faith in Him, let Him do His job, and know that it will be in His time. We must have insight into our own thoughts and how we look and deal with the things around us. Knowing as long as we stay on the path He has led us to, the light will shine brighter than we ever imagined.

62

No need to look back. There is nothing for me in the past. The memories will always linger, nothing is ever completely forgotten. The key would be to focus on all those feel-good memories leaving others to stay far below the surface. Nothing can change what has already happened. Learn and grow from every experience to make each new step better and positive. The moment we can embrace the present and future is when we find out who we are truly supposed to be. There is a way to do just that, find who we are without judgment within. What reaches our soul? Makes us tick? Brings us happiness and peace? Fulfills who we are deep to the core of our being? Purpose? We all have one! We just need to find it. That can be tricky. It was for me. Every person will have a different process and time frame. Best advice I can offer: pray on it and be open-minded to all things and people who cross your path. Give it time because one day your purpose might just smack you in the face when you least expect it.

63

Sometimes I get thoughts in my head about things I would like to see happen. Not negative, nor positive. But then those things do not happen and it brings me down. Makes me think, Satan is putting those hopeful thoughts there knowing what the outcome will be. This is a true eye-opening realization for me. I have had those types of thoughts in my head and when they did not happen, i got really depressed and cried. And that is when I am a target for Satan's ways. Now that I have figured that out, I will no longer be his target.

64

Positive attitude and outlook on life is one of the hardest things I have had to focus on maintaining every moment Satan drops a bomb in my path. Sometimes I see it before it explodes and can dodge it in some manner, not letting any part of it hit me. Other times I see it too late and just get hit by pieces after it explodes. But what hits the hardest is when I step directly on it, shattering a piece of me. It happens to all of us. I believe sometimes we are unaware that it is happening or how to react to each situation.

65

The company we keep plays a big part in the attitude we have at the moment. Being in a negative environment or situation will give us a sense that it is okay to adapt and will manifest negative. But as I am learning daily, I have to be strong enough in my faith that God put me there for a reason. And that reason is to shine a positive light and get the people around me to see light is better than dark. It is my job to help people see that no matter the situation, we *can* find good. Not an easy task. And sometimes we have to do it in a way that is not necessarily direct. As I have been told, it is my job to plant the seed. Once I put the seed there, watering it with positive thoughts and words, it will grow into a beautiful blessing. At that point, blessings will multiply into rays of light the world will not be able to deny.

66

How are you heard?

What do you hear?

Two things to really think about. I learned a long time ago that when speaking to a group of people, they only hear the first 30-60 seconds of what you are saying (not much time). Those people might be listening, but they probably don't hear you. There is a difference. So, the most important information to grab someone's attention needs to be shared within the first minute of you talking. That is not easy. After that, powerful words are what a person will pick out of what you are saying to them just to keep the interest sparked. Each individual word you say needs to hold power. That power needs to be backed by passion you feel and expressed to make that initial spark a flame to draw others in (just like a moth to a flame). As we talk about subjects that excite us, it will show in our body language, tone and energy. People will notice. And the one thing that will stand out even more is the light we shine when our passion and purpose reflect the positive vibrations of God in our lives. Most people will gravitate to light. Light means happy. Happy is positive. And overall, we are all looking for true happiness. It is there. We all just need to embrace it. With our faith, God can do anything. We can do anything with God. We also need to understand God has a plan for us. We don't know what that is. It might not be easy some days to hold on to the light no matter what is thrown in our path, but with faith the size of a mustard seed, God will make the impossible possible. Keep the negative out, let the positive flourish. Life (God) may just surprise you.

67

Times are changing. Of course, change happens with every second, every word, every action. It happens whether we want it to or not. Ultimately, we need to embrace change. Make it a good thing and not something people sometimes dread and see as a negative.

68

There are just some things you cannot change. Whether it is negative or positive, right or wrong, true or false. Words once they are out there, verbal or written, you cannot change them. Words will be remembered. Powerful words will be repeated. Describing feelings you have about anything or anyone will be thought about by yourself or others many times over. Feelings can change, but when put into words they become very powerful, because those words now can be used for good or bad. And this can be a hard lesson to learn. It is a struggle. You want people to know how you feel about them, others, situations, or even about yourself. But when you just throw words out there without much thought, no matter what you say it will be remembered even if they do not totally emulate what it is you were putting out there. So, you debate the right words and whether or not you should put them into existence. Then, do the right thing according to your conversation with God. You think it is the right time, the right words, in the right frame of mind to do so. But the one thing you have to do is be prepared for what comes next, other people's reactions, feelings and words. You think you are ready. You think you know what to expect. You think that whatever happens after it is 'out there' does not matter because at least you had your say. And at times, it may all work out exactly the way you wanted and pictured it would. Other times, your timing might be off and the words will linger there until the timing is right. Then, there will be times where the power of those words are too much and you lose yourself in a way. You said them. You meant them. You cannot take them back. Now what? Wish I had the answer to that right now. But I am learning. I struggle with the realization that when I think I am doing it right and I have put all that effort into making myself aware of what I am doing, the result can be disheartening at times. That is when I have the most faith in the path God has put me on and wait for the outcomes He is working on for me and the purpose I am to fulfill in my life. I might not like it. I might even get a little angry or sad about it. But my reaction to anything needs to reflect the positive outcome I am looking for. So, turning the angriness and sadness into something great and positive is my daily challenge. And I just have to have faith God's plan and purpose for me is greater than anything I could ever imagine. I just have to remember that Satan is going to do everything in his power to sway my thoughts and even cause me to doubt what I am doing or going to do. But God's power is stronger and shines with the light that is never-ending. So, I will stay in the light that never goes away, knowing it can only lead to the greatest outcome ever, God's plan and purpose for me. And God has just that for everyone. All it takes is faith in God!

69

Every day I wake up I question myself. I have never been the confident person who just knows what I am supposed to be doing in my life. Things going on around me change. I get lost in who I think I am supposed to be. We all compare ourselves to others. It is human nature. We base our success on the competition that surrounds us. It is how many of us were raised. It is the way the world looks at happiness. Some might disagree with that, but my perception is just that: success = happiness. I don't think we mean to look at life with such blinders on, but it is learned. Our parents want us to go above and beyond what they did. As a parent, I am sure I did the same things when my children were young. We want them to be the best they can be and to encourage that we compare them to the world and people around them, thinking that will motivate them. When in retrospect, we are possibly setting them up to become more discouraged and unmotivated when they cannot reach a goal as fast as someone else or be as good as another person at something. I think we do this with good intentions. I think we even do this without thinking because it is the way our society has worked for a long time.

Competition gives some people drive to be better. But we need to teach that it is not about being better than another person, it is about being better than you were yesterday. We need to learn how to become our higher selves in everything we do. We need to encourage others to become their higher selves. God never once asked us to compare ourselves to anyone and try to become like them or better than them. He has given each of us a path with a purpose individualized to who we are. We just need to know it is about becoming who we are supposed to be and not what we or others think we are supposed to be. And that is in every aspect of our lives. We have to think about being our best while lifting others to be their best also. Competition is always going to be a thing. As humans, we cannot get around that. Sometimes we will win. Sometimes we will fail. But making sure no matter the outcome of anything that happens to us, we need to shine our light, keep the darkness at bay, and know our higher self is what others are seeing. When they see you shine and be the best you can be with positive words and actions in any situation, they will be encouraged to be their higher self knowing you can win even if you lose sometimes.

70

Beautiful fall day. Clear skies. Bright sun. Keeping my mind positive and clear. Avoiding the chaos that tries to creep in. Wondering where God is going to lead me today. Faith in the job he is doing above anything else. Knowing He is working on me. Always a work in progress.

71

Our past grows as we get older. Think about it. We reflect and think about things we have done, what others have done, and events that have taken place. It can be good when we smile as we think about it. But the times we reflect on our past and we get sad or angry is concerning. Yes, we learn from it. Yes, it is a part of who we have become. Our past is important. But what happens when the past is taken away from our present; and even more important for our future. It is not easy to do, but limit the time you spend in the past. Using our time to focus on the things we need or want to do right now should be priority. Set goals to keep our eyes on the future. We have to use our past to make our future better while living in the present.

72

Love Thyself First

Not a phrase or concept we are used to or even think about a lot of the time. But what it comes down to is if you do not love yourself fully, then it is really difficult to love someone else. Now, I am not saying we do not love others as we are learning to love ourselves. Loving family and friends goes without saying. That is a love that starts early in life. We love those people in our lives differently than that one special person we chose to spend our life with and share ourselves with every day on every level. And to find that person, knowing God put them directly in your path for a reason. The reason might just be to help each other find themselves fully while building something special and unique together. Sometimes it takes another person to make us realize where we have gone wrong in the past while helping us find that true self-love we all search for. It takes time. It takes patience. It takes faith. It even takes lots of discipline to make sure we stay out of the darkness and on the right path of light thru the entire process. That person who we are blessed with by God will always be there. It can all come together into something beyond what could ever have been imagined.

73

We think we know what we want. We think we know what is best. We think we know where we are headed in our lives. We think of lots of things in our lives, but what do we really know? What do we really have control of? The real answer to this deep question is: not much. When you really think about it, you only have control of you. That is the long and short of the story. And because that is the only thing we control, all things we do, say, think, and show the world around us is important. That doesn't mean we have to be serious all the time. It just means we need to be aware of ourselves. Even though we know it is not our job to judge anyone, there are people who will take the time to judge us. (God is our only true judge.) When we are doing our best to shine the light and keep the darkness away, our job is to do the best we can in the light. God is working on us every single second in ways we cannot even imagine. And for that reason, we should be working endlessly for Him. God will always take care of all our needs as long as we have faith knowing He is always on the job. Working for God is not difficult. Reflecting God's goodness thru the way we speak, the actions we demonstrate, and the light and positivity we shine on others and situations we deal with everyday. Not an easy task. Satan will try and stop us. He will throw temptations in our path, toss a dark blanket on us, and put negative thoughts in our heads. We have to remember: if we don't give those things power over us, we break Satan's hold on us. The darkness will be broken and the light has all the power.

74

It is an amazing feeling when someone close to you 'catches the Spirit.' That feeling is even better when it is your child. And I believe it happens at just the right time for that person. As a parent, we can take our kids to church and all the religious activities out there. And there will be times at a young age a child will get it and hold onto it their entire lives. Other situations will cause a person to just not grasp the idea of God and all He really does in our lives. The reasons can be endless as to why anyone out there has not found the Spirit. But when you see and feel someone finally finding that path it is so special. I am talking specifically of my son. At the age of 22, he is finding the light. I would like to think the change in me over the past six months might have something to do with it. Or the amazing friend who helped me also impacted my son with the passion and energy he uses when he speaks about God and spirituality. But then again it could have been the nice girls who invited him to their church. No matter what it was, I am thankful he is on the path of finding God, his purpose and his spirituality. I will continue on my path and encourage him each step he takes on his.

75

Sometimes I try to keep myself in check. Not knowing what to do with the tears as they make their way down my face so unexpectedly. When it happens, I think to myself 'why?' The answer does not come. So I figure if I do not have the answer, God will. And this is when the questions to Him start. Next, when the answers do not pop in front of my face right away, I start to reflect on what is going on around me at the moment. Answers for my tears just are not there. At this point, I have to believe the reason is there, God knows exactly what that reason is, but is not ready to reveal it to me. Now, my faith in Him and the job He is doing in my life is what I want to put my energy into when this happens. God will let me know, in His way, at His time, what it all means. I cannot deny the blessings He has put before me. A good number of those blessings I did not realize their importance until God wanted me too. He does not do anything right in front of us because He knows our faith will show us. God has His ways and reasons. We just have to believe he wants and knows what is best for us always.

76

Knowing but not knowing. That is how I feel. Life keeps throwing me challenges. I take them on. Not allowing anything to stop my dream. Keeping focus on the future while making strides in the present. My prayers are from my heart. Only wanting good for others. I feel my time is coming. God is working on me. In return, I am working for Him. There are times when reality hits, which means my control over anything is very limited. So, when it comes down to getting things done to make my dream a reality, I have to give it everything I can and just pray it is enough to make it my present and future. It is my drive. It is my passion I cannot express enough. I need this more than anything. And it is all in the name of Jesus.

77

Everyday I try desperately not to turn around and look at my past. Even a glimpse causes me to have feelings I do not like to revisit. Knowing it brought me to where I am right now, I have to be thankful for all the things behind me. I did not see all those memories good and bad as blessings from God until recently. I feel we all have things God puts in our path that we absolutely have to go thru to get to where we are supposed to be. If we do not tread thru those muddy waters, we will not realize the difference between good and bad, happy and sad, positive and negative. There will come a time in all our lives where things just fall into place, the planets will align right above our heads, and God's light shines non-stop on us. As the light shines on us, we will let it shine thru us so others cannot miss the difference God's presence makes in our lives. We all make choices, God gives us that ability. When we start making our life choices with a positive mind and God's guidance to stay on the path He has put us on to continue our journey shining the light He provided, we become an extension of all that will be good in the world. And that is what we share and focus our attention on daily.

Other than talking to God many times a day, the biggest blessing on my journey has been finding someone special to share all this with. I was lost in so many ways before I met Jeremy. I had no idea what to do with myself. Packing up my whole life and moving 800 miles was a huge change, but a good one. I was with most of my family again getting the support I had been missing for a while. My family is the best, but long distance support is not enough. (I did have some awesome family members close by, but it was not the same as my parents and my sister. I miss my daughter and her little family who are still in Indiana.) So, here I am in a new state (Texas), a new job (thanks to my uncle), new arrangements for my life knowing it was all good for me. But I was still holding on to things (people) left behind. It took meeting Jeramy and talks about finding purpose, asking for help to move forward, and him not sugar-coating anything. He helped me see. Helped me let go. He helped me find. The connection we have developed is undeniable. My feelings run deep and my gratitude even deeper. We have started something that means so much to both of us. It is our project that has given me the one thing I have been looking for my whole life - true purpose. I am forever thankful to God for answering my prayers and for leading me here. And He led me to Jeremy.

78

So many times, over-thinking life will drown the spirit; especially when we do not get the results when we want or how we want. In a time like this, I try so hard to remember the God Job. It never is about what I want when I want it. God is in control. He knows what is best for us. He knows the outcome of every situation. Our faith and trust in Him should give us peace of mind knowing He only wants good things for us. The more we let go and give God control of all things, the more energy we can spend on shining his light to the world. He is working so hard on our behalf, we have to return the energy and so much more to Him. God does not ask very much of us considering all he does for us. Life can be that simple.

79

Many things influence our love in many different ways. But after reflecting on that thought for a while, my mind started thinking specifically about relationships we have throughout our lives. It starts the day we are born and ends with our last breath. Some relationships just happen. Some short. Some long. Some good. Some not so good. We all learn from the relationships we have, but there are two relationships we have in our lives that most people do not put a lot of thought into and even less effort. And they are definitely the most important relationships we will ever have: #1 with God; #2 with ourselves. These are our never-ending relationships.

Our most precious and loving relationship is with the one who is always with us, never gives up on us, wants only good things for us, and is relentless in His fight for us. He has never let us down. Every step we take in life he is right there with us. He does great things for us even when we do not deserve it. And God only asks for one thing from us: faith! Now, that does require us to shine His light to others. In doing that, I can honestly say life is better and things just fall into good places. Give it a try and you will see how a strong relationship with God gives you more than you ever expected.

Now, think about your relationship with yourself. It has ups and downs. There are a lot of outside forces that impact how we feel about who we are, what we do and how we ultimately deal with life. I believe this may be the most difficult relationship we have in our lives. We are hardest on ourselves when things do not go our way or how we think it should go. What we need to remember - we are a work in progress and have to continue to move forward. Keeping focus on the present and future. Let the past go as lessons learned. We have to learn to become our higher selves each day. That includes every level of our being - physically, emotionally, mentally, and spiritually. When we fall, we must get up, give ourselves a positive pep talk and know we can do anything with hard work and a positive attitude. No matter what the world throws at us, we are capable of catching the ball and making the right play with the no quit attitude we need to hold onto. Keeping the positive thoughts flowing about who we are, what we want to become, while staying on His chosen path will keep the relationship with yourself strong with purpose and drive.

The last relationship we have in our lives is the one that will challenge us the most. The saying goes, "Love thy neighbor as you love yourself."

80

Woke up this morning with a renewed sense of who I am and where I want to be. The sun is shining. My spirit has been lifted above all my insecurities and fears. I know God's plan for me is bigger than I can even imagine. I know this because God's promises are unfailing. The job He is doing gives light and hope to us all. What we do with all of that is key. Satan will do all he can to mask our enlightenment with his darkness. Drawing on all the things that will cast doubt on any situation or small lingering thought in our heads. We do not always recognize this as it is happening. We may even spend time buying into what Satan is selling. At times, it will be easier for us to fall and just sit where we are accepting the cards Satan is dealing us. And the longer we stay there, the more comfortable we get in the dark. But there is no true happiness in the darkness Satan throws over us. Only negative thoughts, actions, and behaviors prosper in the dark. Nothing grows. We grow in light. God's light. There will be times we find ourselves in darkness not knowing how or why we are there. But once the realization hits, get up and remember, no matter how hard we fall, God never leaves us. So many times the fall will cause doubts in who we are and what we are worthy of; that was my most recent fall. But I came to terms with the fact that those doubts are Satan being scared of the light in my heart ready to shine to the world. He wants me to think I can't. But thru God I can do anything. And that makes me worthy of spreading God's light to everyone. I will not let Satan hold me back. I will always get up and move forward with the grace of God in my heart. One day I will stop falling.

81

Being lost in your head. Assuming anything about anyone. Letting uncertainity take over where the certainty of the journey should be. All this is Satan saying, "I will stop the light with all the doubts I can plague your day with."

When this happens, how do we break the pattern? How do we recognize it before it starts? How do we come out of it stronger? How do we keep from hurting someone?

The answer would be, time to go to the closet and ask God to take away the cloud of darkness lingering overhead. Hand Him all we do not understand because Satan is giving us confusion and God will return with clarity.

It can be that simple.

82

There will be days when waking up from a night of dreaming makes you feel down. That is Satan dancing around you at night while you are in your most relaxed state: mind, body, and soul. And if you are doing your best shining God's light in any and all ways you can, Satan will go to all extremes to shut you down. Put doubts in your path so you will turn off to a path he created to keep you away from God. All those mornings we wake up with no motivation to tackle the day, our first thought is, "I just don't want to today." Tears are running down your cheeks because that negative dream was just so real. Satan invaded. When that happens, and you recognize it, rebuke all those thoughts, feelings, and insecurities he placed there overnight. They cannot stay. It is time to deny them any power over you. Have that heart to heart talk with God. Know with the grace and promises God has given us, we have the power to overthrow Satan. His attempt to bring us down will never work. What does work is everything in the name of Jesus and brightening the world with the love of God. Never speak on the negative images Satan places in our dreams. We only need to bring good things into existence with the words we speak. Shine God's light of positivity. And just remember: NOT TODAY SATAN!

83

Something has been on my mind lately. I have taken it to my closet. Waited. Prayed for understanding of myself and the way I do things. I put my heart out there. I have my entire life. It has led to many disappointments. So, I guess I am just not sure where I go wrong, how to change so I don't get hurt and is God giving me answers that I am just not getting. This is where I lose my faith in my abilities to know anything.

84

Talking is the best form of communication. Not texting. Not email. Not Facebook, Instagram, Snapchat, or any other type of social media. Talking has become a lost art. Yes, words are powerful in any form. But when we speak words there is a feeling put behind them. Feelings have been taken out of a lot of things we do and say. People don't want to show feelings because of the reactions they might receive from others. What we all need to remember is…the way we convey things is just as important as the words we use. Positive will result in positive. Negative will result in negative. Waking up positive, the day will be brighter even if it is raining. Waking up negative, the day will feel dark even in the bright sun. It is all about outlook, our attitude, and our reaction in any situation. Take the negative that creeps in directly to your closet, hand it to God, let Him do His work, and you shine because God is on the job. You shine His light. Everything positive is thru God. Everything negative is Satan trying his best to dim our brightness. So, while God is doing all He promises us He will do; we have to make sure we do our part to make the world aware that the good is a representation of God. As a child of God and a lifetime student of His blessings, I am here to say…my faith in the good, positive, bright shining light is everything. Sharing and showing the world the best way I know how is my job. We do not always realize the work He is doing and why, but faith over any kind of fear we might possess is when the Higher Power shines the brightest. And there is power in numbers. The more faith in God, the more positivity in attitude, the more love toward everyone, the more light that shines, the less fear in the world, the less negativity in actions and words, the less power Satan has in our lives. It can happen. I will do my absolute best to make sure my light and positivity shines, because of God, to everyone I meet. One kind word. One smile. One hug. One positive gesture. Can all make a difference.

85

Waking up is the first blessing of the day. Thinking about all the promises a new day has to offer. Knowing God's light will shine even thru the clouds and rain. Feeling the vibrations of positivity. Projecting the rays thru all the cracks. Remembering the job at hand. Forsaking all the false hope in the darkness. The blanket has been lifted. The fear no longer felt. Faith taking over completely. Feet moving forward. Eyes focused on the straight path ahead. Leaving behind the rollercoaster of the past. Keeping it real. Sharing all the beliefs of promises made. Never fading or falling. Shining in eternal light.

86

Trying to understand, maybe what I am not supposed to understand. One moment of clarity followed by endless bouts of confusion. Sometimes it comes down to not really knowing much of what is really true. Living in a world where there are so many doubts. Never really getting to the root of anything.

87

There are times when we are walking our path knowing exactly where we are headed and our purpose is clear. Then, we just stop. Everything gets a bit cloudy. You know there is another path to go down. But, this is the one you have been searching for and refuse to step off of it. And you don't realize you have stopped until a person who knows where you are going points out a change. When that happens, it is time to think about why movement has stopped. The answer does not come to you right away. It is not a negative feeling you have, but the positive light is not shining either. What needs to be fixed? Standing in the middle of my path refusing to look back, unwilling to leave this path I started on, looking forward knowing it is time to take away any doubts or fears and lay them down for God. It is time to forget what I think should be. Knowing that I am blessed and forever grateful for the awesome changes that have taken place in my life over the past year. Keeping the positivity in my attitude, on my face, and especially in my voice so others can feel the light I want to shine every moment of every day. Time to know that I am not supposed to really know until I do. Everything in time with patience and positivity.

88

Missing the target of where I need to be. Time to take aim. Be patient with myself. Jesus please help me calm the storm and battle going on inside. I have to let go of all I cannot control and trust in all You control for us. Know that Your control is more than I could ever imagine.

89

Power. Passion. Strength. Focus. Control. All important. I want possession of all these things. But I am learning, only with Jesus holding my hand can I have any of those. I cannot do anything alone. I have tried. I have fallen. I have cried many tears. And it was because I wanted to do it all myself. It was a long walk to figure out I cannot do any of the things in life alone. I would like to say this just came to me one day. Not true. The reality is, it took many conversations with Jeremy, nights with little sleep seeking wisdom and understanding from God, tears of frustration, and finally the brick wall I kept hitting started to crack in places. The light peeked thru to lift the darkness of confusion. It is a process, as is life. The wall will slowly crumble as I gain understanding of my place and follow the path to fulfill this purpose God is leading me to, every moment.

90

Why am I so insecure? How is it that I am so unsure of myself? I always put others first. I try to make sure those around me are happy and taken care of. I don't think I have ever asked for too much from anyone. Since starting my journey of purpose, I have found my spiritual side and embraced it. Shining light and sharing positive in everything that happens. Words are power - what is spoken (and written) and the way those words are expressed, meaning tone and volume. Misspeaking can lead to misunderstanding. Something we all need to work on daily. There are times when emotions will take over. Controlling emotions is challenging, but needs to be one thing we think about when others react to what we say. This is what we all struggle with, we just don't always know it.

Lately my emotions are overflowing and my control is slipping. It is like a downpour of rain flooding everything inside me and I cannot get a grip. I pray. I take it to my closet knowing I cannot let the floodgates burst open. It would be too much for me and anyone around me. There are some things I cannot let out for many reasons. I am sure lately I have let too much out. I pray for God to give me the right words at the right time, strength in all things He wants me to do, and wisdom to just know. I want to be the best I can possibly be. I want to show those around me something different. My life is about what I can do for others. And will continue to be. I just want to be loved for once where who I am means something to someone. I want to be part of something special.

91

Life is unexpected. No matter how hard we try, there is no way to know what each moment will bring. We plan, but nothing will ever come out perfect. No such thing. 'Live in the moment' is a statement thrown out all the time. Easier said than done for some. It just comes down to - we never know from minute to minute what will take place in our lives. We just have to do the best we can with every moment we are given.

I have been trying really hard to remember that because it is one of my challenges. Getting stuck in my thoughts and the feelings of not knowing what to do is why I spend time talking to God, more lately than I ever have. It has always been about finding happiness with someone. Wanting that special love unconditionally from the one my heart cannot stop feeling so much for. I pray about it. I ask for wisdom to know if I should hold on and be patient. It is the not knowing right now that makes the tears fall and my heart hurt.

92

Keeping our eyes focused on the path to God is not as hard as some want to make it. True happiness is found in the light of God. It is not just about knowing and believing. The highest emotion of love should be our feelings and actions to and for God. Unconditional. Unwavering. Because the only complete true love and most important relationship is with God. And if it is not, think about what it absolutely should be. He knows us better than we know ourselves. He is always with us. He always listens. His love for all of us is unconditional. What He does is greater than any man. He works for us more than we are even aware. Great things take place because we feel God's light and shine it to others. Nothing is more powerful than our love for God (and His love for us). And when we take the time each day to strengthen that loving relationship, life is different in so many ways. Life is better when God is in control.

93

Many times we have conversations with people and as we listen we take it all in. Sometimes a lesson is learned right away. Other times the lesson will come later when something triggers it. At that point, it just clicks and you are enlightened. Could be something small. Or a huge life changing mindset. Any type of enlightenment is a step forward. And it will be different for everyone.

94

Anything can and will change in a moment of time

95

Hidden messages of God and faith in our everyday encounters we do not realize are providing us with unrecognized light. The same can be true for Satan's unrelenting cloak of negative masked in what we initially take as possibly good. Think about that. If it is wrapped with pretty paper and a bow, it must be a great gift. But putting a bow on a pile of poop does not make it anything but what it is. Television, music, social media, and even people right in front of you can project so many things to you from so many angles. This is when we need to know if it is God speaking to us or a red flag waving.

96

It is very difficult to find a special connection with anyone these days. God places people in our path for many different reasons. The funny and interesting part is we may not understand God's reasons for a very long time. Rarely is it an instantaneous draw that continues over long periods. Life is full of changes - moment to moment. God's path for us may not line up with the way we think or feel the plan should go. And there are times where it is just not about us as individuals. It is a bigger picture God has not revealed completely to us. Timing. Patience. Accepting. Believing. Faith. Knowing each person we come in contact with is important as an individual. The contact we have with each person no matter how brief or long, is of importance in some way. Make it count for both of you

.Now, if you are lucky enough to find a special person where the connection is instant and lasting then God has a big purpose for that bond. It is not easy to find that and sometimes harder to keep it in today's world. Many factors are going to play on that relationship. Satan has a way of swaying God's plans. We do not always see it coming or recognize it as it is happening. But when the spirit of God is the focus, that bond and the journey ahead will be unwavering. Bumps will happen. Satan will do his best to make cracks into Grand Canyon size holes. But with the grace of God and the job He relentlessly works, two people shining and sticking together to make sure the will of God, the journey ahead, and the bigger picture can be revealed. Don't let go of the bond God created to make His light undeniable. Find it. Keep it. Grow it. God's reasons are there. Faith will carry it thru.

97

So unsettled…the atmosphere around me. Following the path of light and positivity. Finding my way to days of sharing and shining. Looking to make a real difference in a world of uncertainty and searching. The wider we open our eyes and hearts the brighter we shine with God's light. Now is a special time because as the light shines brighter the power grows as we ultimately wait. What are we waiting for you may wonder…

98

Today is April 16, 2022, the day between Good Friday and Easter. I woke up with something on my mind. I could not pinpoint what it was at first. So, I went about my morning rituals. Get up, get moving. Then, I got on Facebook and everything hit me. There are many posts about Easter. Now, I know why I feel a little off. Many posts detail Jesus' suffering - all He was put thru on Good Friday. What people did to Him to make His suffering beyond what any typical man could endure. And it always makes me cry. To think about how one extraordinary man could literally take on the weight of the world. He felt everything. He heard everything. He never gave up. Even in death He did not give up. Because He came back. He came back to the people who caused His pain. He came back to His believers. He came out of that tomb to show us God stands on His promises. God can and will do the impossible. God has a plan for all of us. And we all have a purpose. If Jesus' purpose was to endure all of that then come back to show us the truth of God's word, then we must shine the light of God to everyone. Let everyone know - He is the WAY, the TRUTH, and the HOPE for EVERYTHING. Undeniable.

99

There are going to be days in our lives when we may not be able to explain how we feel, why we feel that way, or how to move forward to get those brighter days. On these kinds of days, it is more important to have those in depth talks with God in our closets. Know He listens to every word. Know He feels everything we feel. Know His deep concern for us in moments like this. Faith He will help us rise from these times we don't have the answer. He will shine His light to bring us out of the darkness Satan has thrown over us. We have hope and love thru God. He promises us that. He stands on all His promises. And when we need that reminder, all we need to do is open our hearts and especially our minds to what He has to say to us. God does not want us to get stuck under the blanket Satan tries to cover our light with. Seeking Him in these times Satan is working his hardest to dim our light, knowing that God is working harder and is stronger. This is where we have to let go of everything and give it to God. When our faith in all He can do shines, the darkness goes away. When the darkness goes away, nothing can stop our lights from shining on everything in our path ahead. Look up and just know.

100

Words spoken by even the most trusted person in your life are only words unless backed up by actions. I learn that more each and every day. Sometimes I think about it and it even makes me a little sad. Not one person on this earth is perfect. We can strive each day to do our best, but perfection can only be reached by God and when we come face to face with Him.

101

~~~~~~

Spending my time lately really trying to figure out how things are going to come together. All of those thoughts have me on edge just a little, but I do not want to let on to anyone what is really going on with me. A few things come to mind as all those lingering 'where is my life really going' thoughts hang over my head. The first: Let go and let God. Knowing I have control of nothing outside myself. I can only do what I can do myself. So, I need to put my focus on my words, my actions, my motivation, my abilities, and my strengths. And work on those things to move forward. The second: Take it to my closet. God already knows. But knowing I can bring it all to Him in my words and express myself knowing He always listens and lightens my load gives me hope for all good things meant to happen. The timing is His. The plan is His. The will to follow the path and take the journey with God as my guide is all on me. So standing on my faith as He stands on His promises gives me all the perspective I need knowing life will be full of light, love, and true purpose. The time is before me. I will stand and just know.

102

My closet is the only place to be right now. So many things thrown at me today from every direction. The only one to turn to in moments when we have no control over anything going on is our greatest friend and counselor, God. He is the One who will help guide any decision we face. I thought I had an idea of where I saw my life going, but many things have been brought to my attention today and it set off a flow of thoughts and questions. It was a little bit like a flood gate breaking. No control over anything at the moment. Putting my reactions on hold to all going on. Let go and let God.

103

When I am feeling completely alone, with no one next to me and no one to talk to, I have to sit and remember You are always with me. Getting lost in my head, my heart aching and longing for someone to just give me a hug, I look up and know your arms are always around me. The tears start to fall so I go to my closet knowing we need to talk. You know my heart. You know my thoughts. But I have to let You know in words of my own. I know it is not always about me when I am feeling like this. I know You are working on all of us. I know how important it is for me to share all You are doing. And when I am flooded with all of these overwhelming emotions, it is not You or me. It is Satan putting doubt in myself, trying to dim my light, keeping me from the job I need to be doing. This is when I need to be still and wait. You will give me the guidance I need. Be still. Be patient. And never give Satan the satisfaction of pulling me off my path. I may need to take a break, have a seat on my path, and rest for a time while God is at work, I will never stray from the way He is leading me. Never again will I fear the path God has put before me. I only have faith in God grabbing my hand to help me stand to continue my walk with Him in His time. Patience, faith, and knowing.

104

The time has arrived. Eyes open. Heart full. Words powerful. Lights bright. Thoughts positive. Everything is falling into place to share the love and possibilities God is raining on us. There is absolutely no way we are going to lose this battle. Our weapons are bigger and stronger than the opposition. And when we stand together in the name of Jesus nothing will be able to stop the passion behind our words, light, actions, and change in the way we do life. It is not about a place. It is not about one day. It is not about a leader on earth. It is about a bond that is unbreakable between ourselves and GOd. THen, sharing and bonding with others as testimonies are shared and we are touched by the Spirit. It may take some time to make it all come together. God has a plan. Timing is everything. Patience and persistence is key.

105

I am at a loss this morning. Slight confusion about the words and actions of someone in my life. Not understanding. It is definitely something I have no control over. And I know I have been told over and over not to trust man because there are too many factors on earth to influence and have effects on what man does and says. Many years of being lied to and getting hurt, is enough for me to know the only real trust I need to have is in the power of God. Only He prevails with honesty, truth, and righteousness. He will always be there when I need Him. He has given me no reason to doubt Him because He never breaks a promise. So, when it comes down to it, I must trust God to bring the right people into my life and accept He will let me know when and what to do, being patient and keeping Him first in everything every day.

106

Many times we try to do the right things for the people we love the most and It just does not work out. It is a harsh reality to come to terms with. You hurt because they hurt. You feel helpless because you know there is nothing you can do to fix anything that is going on with them. And there is my problem. It is so much worse when it is your child. Makes it even more difficult when you feel you are to blame. I have spent a lot of my life trying to do the right things to keep those around me happy or less worried about everything. I failed doing that for my children. And have learned that only God has control of things and I do not. I will never question my faith in God and all I know He can do. I know God can do more in 5 minutes that I can do in five years. A friend shared that with me. And I know it is so true. I have been a witness to that. And I do know that I cannot fix anything for anyone else. All I can do is go to my closet and give it all to God. Let go and let God.

107

Everything can change in just one moment. And you might not ever see it coming. I am learning to trust everything the Good Lord puts in my path.

108

Trying to find my way. Looking up for strength and guidance. Always wanting to take care of everyone the best I know how. At this moment, looking to get enough done to be with the man who has come into my life and captured my heart with not just his words, but more importantly his actions. I did not see this coming. I was most definitely not looking for this to happen. It is just amazing how life can change in an instant. No warning. No expectations. And everything happens all at one time. So much, so many directions, it has all changed. Trying to find a balance. I have faith God has a plan for me. I don't want to mess up. I know the control is not mine. Moving forward to make it work.

109

As we get older, simple is a goal. Finding peace and positivity in all we do. Striving to help others find those things too.

110

～～～

Life is an on-going work in progress!

There will always be ups and downs. Challenges will drop right in our path with no warning. But we can be prepared for anything by standing in the light of God. Faith knowing God is with us always. He knows us better than we know ourselves. He created us. He has made promises to us. He made the ultimate sacrifice for us. And once all that sinks in, our very first love must be God. He can do anything. He has done the impossible. And He will continue to shower us with amazing blessings. God has written the playbook. He knows exactly what is going to happen before it happens. I realize that concept is very difficult to believe because we all know there is bad out there in the world. Satan has his hand in this world causing many to have doubts on the Glory God gives us. He wants to plant the negative to get us to not believe, lose faith and turn our backs on God. Light is better than darkness. Happiness trumps sadness. And standing on our faith in God and all the blessings we know about and especially the ones we don't is the most amazing feeling when every day the light shines. We have choices. God gave us freewill. Our freewill should be used to show our gratitude and love to the One who only wants what is best for us in every sense. It is written. It is spoken about. It is a way of life. Speaking positive into our lives changes every sense we have: physical, emotional, mental, and especially spiritual. It reaches us beyond anything else. It makes life better. Positive faith shining brighter than the sun makes life beyond amazing. Speaking about and sharing with others makes it even better. God speaks to us in many ways. We have to learn to recognize His "words". If we don't know for sure, we can ask. His love for us is unconditional, and He will give us the answers.

111

Knowing when the right things are happening for the very right reason. Knowing God is taking care of all we need and not worrying about the next step. Knowing He is next to us every second of every minute of every day. As a child, that concept was lost on me. I often wondered how He could be, listen, and take care of everyone all the time. And as my friend reminds me often, I think too literal. As I have gotten older and met someone to help me grasp my true spiritual side, I finally get it. I do not ever remember hearing as a kid in church "God can make the impossible, possible." And if I did hear it, I did not get it at the time. I missed so much when I was younger in church. But timing (God's timing) is everything. And there, most definitely, is where my journey took me to this point of really grasping one small spiritual concept at a time. It brought me peace and strength when I needed it most. And revealed a purpose I never knew I had or needed.

112

~~~~~~~~

God has His reasons, His timing, His plans for each of us. Not everything is going to go the way we want them too. In fact, nothing will go exactly the way we want, because it is not about what we want. It is about what God's plans are for us. Those special plans are not always easy to understand when they start to play out, but as long as we remember God stands on His promises to us and we stand in His light, everything will fall into the right place at the right time. And if we accept and take all God puts before us, then use all He gives us to glorify Him and shine the light to everyone, we will just feel it all changing. When the light of God shines, the blessings start raining down. Light and rain will show us the amazing works of God because a rainbow will appear leading us to the pot of gold. That very pot of gold is the riches of our eternal life with Him.

113

Two Forces coming together for the greater good. That is the only way I can describe watching the end of season 3 of Cobra Kia. It got me thinking about the many ways we are all different.

Thoughts Feelings Actions Reactions
The way we see things in general.

But one thing we have to realize and come together on, is there is only one Satan with many faces. And we must come together against him, against evil, against negative, against darkness. As I sit here outside looking at the beautiful sunshine, amazing blue sky, listening to the birds and feeling the cool breeze of the morning time in Indiana, I feel energized. I feel peace. I feel positive. I see all possible, thru God and the greatness (vastness) He puts right in front of us every day. See the light. Moment to moment life changes. The control is not ours. Knowing and giving control to God in all situations (moments) can give us that ultimate peace and purpose He is showing us. Only good comes from God. Negative comes from Satan. What do you choose?

114

~~~

Listening, hearing, and understanding are all very different things. You can do one or all of them depending on what your intentions are. Maybe that sounds a little strange, but take a minute to think about it...

Now, think about the ways we 'communicate' with each other. That would include the above mentioned plus our actions, reactions, body language and words we speak. It is not just about spoken words - it is about the whole package. I think about that every time I talk to someone, especially when they are telling me their story. I want to take it all in, react in the right way, and keep my words positive. Not always the easiest thing to do. With practice and true genuine interest in what someone is saying, it comes easier every time we do it. I have learned everyone's story is unique to who they are because of where they have been, how they played the cards they were dealt, their perception of it all, and where they see themselves going. Even if two people go thru similar experiences, guaranteed the way each comes out of it in the end is going to be determined by perception and reactions. We are different in these aspects. But if we put our spirit, our light, and our faith in God of all possible ahead of any thought or reaction to any and all situations that we are faced with, the end results will be far greater than we could ever imagine.

115

Day in and day out there is no preparing for all that goes on in our lives. We are told at one time or another:

"Prepare for the unexpected"
"Expect the best, but prepare for the worst"
"Life is short make the most of every moment"

And so many more little words of wisdom we heard and passed on. For the most part all those sayings are very true.

116

At times life does not make much sense. It can feel like things are crashing all around you, and maybe they are. This is when you must stop and reflect on where your heart is, where your mind is, and where your focus is. The only way to do those things and be able to find the right answers is to take them all to your closet. All your questions, all your emotions, all your thoughts and lay them at God's feet. Let your faith in Him take over all that is clogging your light. Faith that He will provide us the answers and wisdom we seek in all situations. When we give it to God, we must not worry about when or how He will answer. He is the God of all things possible. He has shown us time and time again He can do more in 5 minutes than we can do in 5 years. His promises are strong. Our faith in Him is all we need. Then, just know it will be done.

117

When do we know things are real and never going to leave? It is many times that things are not permanent. A lot of people use that when things are not going well. They say just wait and it will change. That can even be true for good things. Life is full of ups and downs. Life is what we make of it. Hold on to the good times. You never know which way the wind is going to blow. Focus on the positive. Keep your light shining. Speak positive and positive will happen. All this had to do and revolve around God of all things possible. No matter what is going on in life: good, bad, or indifferent, our focus must be on what God is doing for us, with us, and around us. The devil will try his best to sway our focus, our faith, our purpose, and our path. We must stand strong on all the promises God made. He is the One who has shown us miracles in the midst of our chaos. And He will never disappoint us. He is caring. He is understanding. He is forgiving. He stands thru everything. He loves us so much, He sacrificed His son to save us, to prove to us, to give us hope, to show us His light is where we need to be always. In His light, we shine. And when we shine, our days are better. We must look at everything in the light of God. Understanding, strength, and peace is what we find in that light. The love and light of God are things that will never be taken from us.

118

Sometimes things come to light in unexpected ways. A person's true colors will show in ways that may just surprise you. And when your heart cracks a little because of that, all your thoughts and feelings change. Maybe not a lot, but just enough for you to question a person's true thoughts and feelings about you. Actions say so much, and lack of actions says even more. Words have more power than most of us even realize. "Words will never hurt me" is what we said to each other as kids. I am not sure kids still use that, but I am here to say, that is so not true. Words have more power than most give credit. And when negative words are said about you that are not true, it hurts and that feeling lingers. It is worse when things are said by a friend who you have given so much to, gone out of your way for, and never questioned his word. When this happens, the vision changes. And feelings of hurt take over. I never saw it coming. Now, turning to God for understanding.

119

I keep thinking about how to let God's words in and keep Satan's out. Letting go of the way that I want to think, giving up the control I want to have, and making my strength faith in the good, the positive, the light of Our God. It is the only way to go. The one thing that comes to mind now is making faith my super-power and words my weapons to spread love, peace, hope, and shine God's light for the whole world to know the way to make the impossible possible. Once it is shared, seen, and felt there is no denying the only way to get things done right is thru God. He can do anything and everything at any time, anywhere every single day. And what we must learn is God has given each of us gifts to share with the world in some form. We have to learn to use them. We have to share them all in the name of Jesus. Once we all focus our energy on the positive, let those vibrations flow, everything gets better, the light is undeniable because people will see it, feel it, and want to share with others.

120

Yesterday, my spirit was elevated. My light was shining so bright. Every word I spoke made positive. I made plans for more of the same today. I got myself on a high I wanted to share with everyone. Then, it happened. Satan saw my light and did everything in his power to put it out. I kept my eyes up, my tongue in check, and words in the spirit. But he kept at it. My day job did not turn out the way I had hoped for. My ex decided to spit words of hate at me which I did not respond with anything other than enlightened words he was not expecting. At one point, tears filled my eyes. I felt deflated. Deep down I knew God has a plan, reasons I did not understand yet, and Satan was trying to keep me from my spiritual purpose. I spoke to a few ladies at a store I frequently visit, and we spoke in the spirit. That helped so much. And then, I had a conversation with a man who has come into my life and showed me a happiness I have never felt before. He listens. We discuss. We are a team. Partners in life. He encourages me in ways no one ever has. He is a blessing in my life. And he gives me hope for a future of happiness. He is there to lift me up and make me see life a little differently. I know I have many things to look forward to. He tells me: "one day at a time." Being 800 miles away from me right at the moment is not easy, but his unconditional true love is something I have never experienced in a relationship outside of my family. God brought him into my life for a reason. And I am thankful. I know every step forward with God showing me the positive and leading me to something so real, all good things are possible. So on days when everything seems to go wrong because Satan sees my light shining and he wants to put it out, I will focus on only the positive going on around me knowing God stands on all His promises and makes all possible. And I stand on my faith in Him and all the blessings in my life. To the people who lift me when I cannot lift myself. God is amazing in all He does for us and His timing of what we need at the moment.

121

There will come a time when our thoughts, our passions, our priorities, our outlook on life change. The people who play important roles in our lives change for many reasons. We perceive and view life differently. And as long as we are moving forward on the path God led us to shine our lights and project positive vibrations, all those changes are good. There is a song being played on the radio that has a lyric about God always moving. We cannot stay in one place and expect to grow, spiritually. I can attest to this. My spiritual growth started a very long time ago, but I did not fully embrace that part of me until I met someone who really showed me how. Now, I am starting to spread my wings spiritually. It feels amazing. I am learning we all have different ways to express and do things. And we need to be open-minded and willing to see the big picture of life. It helps us grow. It gives us the opportunity to listen and communicate clearly. It gives us time to share and come together loving all those around us.

Conclusion

The words in this book describe my journey over the span of a year. And this is just the beginning. Every person's journey is going to be different. But just remember, we are never truly alone in it. Sharing this with you is the biggest blessing for me. I thank God every single day.

Printed in the United States
by Baker & Taylor Publisher Services